IQ and Psychometric Test Workbook

IQ and Psychometric Test Workbook

Essential preparation for verbal, numerical and spatial aptitude tests, and personality tests

Philip Carter

KoganPage

LONDON PHILADELPHIA NEW DELHI

First published in Great Britain and the United States in 2005 by Kogan Page Limited
This edition 2011
Reprinted 2011, 2012 (twice), 2014 (three times), 2015 (three times)

2nd Floor, 45 Gee Street
London EC1V 3RS
United Kingdom
www.koganpage.com

1518 Walnut Street, Suite 1100
Philadelphia PA 19102
USA

4737/23 Ansari Road
Daryaganj
New Delhi 110002
India

© Philip Carter 2005, 2011

The right of Philip Carter to be identified as the author of this work has been asserted by him in accordance with the Copyright, Designs and Patents Act 1988.

ISBN   978 0 7494 6261 1
E-ISBN   978 0 7494 6262 8

British Library Cataloguing-in-Publication Data

A CIP record for this book is available from the British Library.

Library of Congress Cataloging-in-Publication Data

Carter, Philip J.
    IQ and psychometric test workbook / Philip Carter.
        p. cm.
    Originally published: London ; Sterling, VA : Kogan Page, 2005.
    ISBN 978-0-7494-6261-1 – ISBN 978-0-7494-6262-8   1. Intelligence tests.   2. Personality tests.
    3. Self-evaluation. I. Title.
    BF431.3.C3618 2011
    153.9'3–dc22

                                                                                                        2010033140

Typeset by Graphicraft Limited, Hong Kong
Print production managed by Jellyfish
Printed and bound in Great Britain by Ashford Colour Press Ltd

Contents

Introduction

This aim of this book is for readers to obtain a greater understanding of psychometric testing by means of practice tests in which readers will be able to familiarize themselves with the type of questions they are likely to be faced with when taking such tests.

The book, which is a companion volume to my earlier title *IQ and Psychometric Tests* (Kogan Page, 2011), concentrates on aptitude testing in three main areas – verbal aptitude, numerical aptitude and spatial (visual/perceptual) aptitude – as well as personality tests to examine temperamental traits.

In addition to providing valuable practice on the type of tests likely to be encountered, the book also explains in detail the type of questions found within these tests, together with some of the thought processes that should be applied. For all tests, detailed explanations of the answers, where applicable, are provided, together with feedback to readers in the form of performance assessment.

The feedback provided will give the opportunity to identify strengths and weaknesses. This will enable readers to build on their strengths and work at improving their performance in areas of weakness.

There are also comprehensive notes on adopting the right approach to psychometric testing, and tips on how to prepare for a test and how to approach the taking of the test in the right frame of mind.

As in the case of many new experiences, one of the main keys to success is understanding. By obtaining an understanding of the testing process and its purpose, and by adopting a positive attitude towards this type of testing, it is possible to increase your performance when undergoing psychometric testing.

Preparation for testing

Psychometric tests are basically tools used for measuring the mind. The word 'metric' means *measure* and the word 'psycho' means *mind*. There are two types of psychometric tests, which are usually used in tandem by employers. These are aptitude tests, which assess your abilities, and personality questionnaires, which help build up a profile of an individual's characteristics and personality.

An ability test is designed to measure maximum performance and potential in a number of areas. These abilities can be measured separately, or combined to give an assessment of overall general ability. Often tests are constructed so that they relate to a specific job or skill and assess things such as perceptual speed or mechanical reasoning. Examples of ability tests are general intelligence tests (IQ tests), knowledge-based attainment tests, and aptitude tests, which test the ability to use knowledge. Personality questionnaires are usually administered without a set time limit and the questions have no right or wrong answers.

It is essential that you approach any test confidently and systematically and without getting into a state of panic. As well as carrying out some research into the type of question you may encounter, it is also important that you are in the right frame of mind. It is natural to have some anxiety symptoms prior to taking any kind of test. In fact, a certain degree of anxiety, or butterflies in the stomach, can be helpful in any test situation because it shows that you are concentrating and focusing your energies on the task ahead. On the other hand, if you are overly anxious, this is likely to affect your performance adversely.

When preparing for the actual test it may be helpful to bear in mind as many of the following points as possible:

- Try to get a good night's sleep beforehand. This will help to ensure you arrive at the test centre in as calm a state of mind as possible.

- Do not take the test on an empty stomach. If you feel too nervous to have a big breakfast before an early morning test, have a light snack.

- Make sure you know the directions to the test centre beforehand and have a trial run a few days before if necessary. Arrive in good time for the test and, above all, don't dash in at the last minute flustered and wound up. Allow extra time to arrive at the test centre in case of any possible delays in your journey. Also, make sure you use the toilet facilities if necessary prior to commencement of the test.

- If you wear glasses or a hearing aid do not forget to take them along. Tell the instructor if you have any disabilities that you feel he or she should know about.

- Make sure you are comfortable.

- If you have a practice or instructional stage before the actual test, pay attention to this very carefully, irrespective of how trivial or obvious some of the points being made by the administrator may appear. At this stage do not be afraid to ask any questions of the administrator. Test administrators follow a standard set of instructions, which is necessary to ensure that everyone takes the test under exactly the same conditions, so listen carefully to the administrator's brief and ask any questions prior to the commencement of the test.

- Read the instructions to each test carefully.

- Avoid *skimming* – looking through the test to seek out all the questions first for which you know the answer. Apart from wasting time, this can be a confidence-destroying exercise if at first glance you think there are only a few questions that you are able to answer. It is far more effective to work through the questions systematically and methodically one at a time.

- Bear in mind that usually the more questions you answer the higher you score, so work as *quickly*, but as *carefully*, as possible.

- Do not spend too long on any one question; either come back to it at the end of the test, if there is time remaining, or make an educated or intuitive guess (subject to the following proviso).

- Usually, you are not penalized for getting an answer wrong, other than not getting a mark for answering it correctly. However, on some tests, particularly if the questions are multi-choice, the marker may apply a guessing factor. For example, on a test of 25 questions where each question has five choices you would, on average, be expected to get five questions correct if you guessed the answer to them all. If, however, the marker then made a one-point deduction for every five questions you answered incorrectly (in this case 20 questions) you would end up having four points deducted, which would leave you with only one point. You should, therefore, ask the instructor prior to commencement of the test whether there is to be any penalty for incorrectly answered questions, as it is your entitlement to be given this information.

- Focus your attention on the job in hand – avoid all distractions.

- Don't panic! If you panic you may begin to lose confidence in your own ability to answer the most obvious questions. Although it is easy to say 'Don't panic', when faced with any task or situation that involves pressure it is not that easy to do. *Too much to do and too little time in which to do it* is a scenario that is familiar to most of us. If, however, you are able to discipline yourself to approach any such circumstance in a logical, calm and structured fashion, it is surprising how the task becomes much less daunting.

- Work quickly and accurately, but do not rush.

- Make sure you put your answers in the correct place.

- Double-check each answer quickly.

- Do not be afraid of any one type of question.

- Bear in mind that in many tests questions progressively get harder.

- Although your main focus of attention and concentration should be on the questions themselves, also be aware of the time and try to pace yourself.

- If you have time to spare at the end of the test, use the extra time to have a quick review of your answers.

- Some tests have very strict time limits to ensure that many people cannot complete all the questions in the time available. Other tests have more relaxed time limits. In the latter case the questions may be quite difficult, or start off easy and get progressively harder, and in the case of such tests the emphasis may be on how many questions you answer correctly rather than how fast you work. Generally tests fall somewhere between these two extremes and there will be a time limit set that will enable most people to complete the test. Nevertheless you should still work as quickly as possible but without rushing.

- Your score is usually interpreted in comparison to the scores obtained by previous test takers. Psychological tests in general are designed so that, on average, people in the group they are intended for will get approximately 50 per cent correct. You should not, therefore, be alarmed if you cannot answer some of the questions, or if you think you have answered some of them incorrectly.

Online testing

There is a current trend towards tests being administered over the internet. Typically you will be sent a user name and password by email and will log on using the address supplied in the email. After logging on, the computer will take you through the instructions and the sample questions before administering the tests question by question. This procedure is particularly common for tests of typical performance (personality tests) where the security of the questions is not of paramount importance and where no time limits are involved. Before taking such a test it is advisable to request a telephone number and contact name in case there are questions or issues you wish to raise.

When asked to take a test by internet please ensure you have, or have access to, a computer that meets the operating system and browser software requirement specified by the tester, and that you will be able to work on the test in a quiet, interruption-free zone for the duration of the test.

Note

A properly validated test is standardized after having been given to a large number of individuals. This procedure establishes the average score, or norm, for each test; for example, on an IQ test the norm would be 100.

As the practice tests that follow have been newly compiled for this book and are not, therefore, standardized, an actual assessment cannot be given. However, a guide to assessing your performance for each test is provided.

CHAPTER 1

Verbal aptitude

The definition of 'verbal aptitude' is the capacity for general lexical skills: the understanding of words and the ability to use them effectively.

Because mastery of words is seen by many as having in one's possession the ability to produce order out of chaos, it is argued that command of vocabulary is a true measure of intelligence.

Verbal abilities include reading, writing and communicating with words. Verbal reasoning tests are designed to measure basic verbal abilities and typically include spelling, grammar, word meanings, completing sentences, synonyms and antonyms. Such tests are widely used in intelligence testing.

Verbal intelligence is, therefore, a measurement of your capacity to use language in order to express yourself, comprehend written text and understand other people. The practice exercises contained in this section test basic verbal aptitude in a number of separate areas including synonyms, antonyms, analogy, odd one out and verbal comprehension.

Whilst there is no substitute for practising on actual tests, there are certain useful strategies that may be adopted when approaching verbal aptitude tests:

- Read each question carefully, concentrating on each word, avoiding the tendency to skip from word to word. In everyday life we may have developed the habit of reading through reports or newspaper articles quickly in order to pick out the general meaning of a sentence or paragraph. When reading a question or a set of test instructions this technique of speed reading should be avoided, as it is necessary to focus your concentration on each single word in order to ensure the test instructions and each question within the test are fully appreciated and understood.

● When you are uncertain of an answer, or the meaning of a word, eliminate first the options that you feel sure to be incorrect; then from the reduced list of options remaining choose the one that you feel looks most right. Often this intuitive approach will lead to the correct choice.

● Although this is a speed test, do not panic! Take the time to read each word carefully. There are usually no trick questions; however, occasionally a list of options may contain similar-sounding or similar-looking words as a distraction or to add a certain degree of confusion to your train of thought. For example, the following is just a very brief sample of words frequently confused in correspondence and sometimes conversation:

accept:	to take, admit, believe
except:	leave out, exclude
advice:	noun: opinion given
advise:	verb: to give an opinion, recommend
affect:	verb: to act on, to influence
effect:	verb: to bring about; noun: result
amount:	how much?
number:	how many?
biannual:	twice a year
biennial:	every two years
cloth:	fabric
clothe:	to dress
coarse:	rough
course:	i) direction of movement; ii) division of a meal; iii) golf or race course
continual:	frequent, repeated
continuous:	unbroken, connected

dual:	twofold
duel:	an arranged fight
envelop:	verb: to surround
envelope:	noun: gummed container for a letter
hear:	listen to
here:	in this place
its:	possessive case of 'it' – 'the bird built its nest'
it's:	contraction of 'it is' or 'it has' – 'it's raining heavily'
loose:	not tight
lose:	suffer loss
moral:	of good conduct
morale:	spirit of fortitude
personal:	individual, private
personnel:	staff employed
principal:	chief, head of school, sum of money
principle:	fundamental truth
stationary:	standing still
stationery:	writing materials
their:	belonging to them
there:	in that place
they're:	contraction of 'they are'
who's:	contraction of 'who is' or 'who has' – 'who's the lady in the red dress?'
whose:	possessive case of 'who' – 'whose dog just barked at the postman?'

The use of punctuation too is a frequent cause for confusion, of which perhaps the most common example is the apostrophe, the uses of which are as summarized below:

1 as a contraction, for example *it's* ('it is'), *don't* ('do not'), *isn't* ('is not'), *you're* ('you are') – which should not be confused with 'your';

2 to indicate possession, for example: the child's toy, the children's games, the Writers' and Artists' Association.

Common misuse of the apostrophe is in the use of plurals, for example Smith's Butcher's Shop (which should read Smith's Butchers Shop), and in the use of pronouns, for example 'its hot outside' (which should read 'it's hot outside') and 'the wedding party made it's way to the reception' (which should read 'the wedding party made its way to the reception').

It is also advisable to bear in mind that some words in the English language that are identical in sound and spelling have quite different meanings. Three examples of the very many such words are:

- *list:* i) catalogue, register, index; ii) lean, tilt, slant;

- *temple:* i) a place for worship; ii) part of the head;

- *scale:* i) crust, overlay, layer; ii) balance; iii) calibration, progression; iv) climb, ascend.

Before taking any verbal aptitude test it is advisable to obtain prior understanding of the type of questions that may be encountered, and the following are typical examples of the type of vocabulary questions used in IQ tests:

- *Synonyms.* A synonym is a word having a similar meaning to another in the same language. For example, synonyms of the word 'correct' are in one sense 'accurate' or 'exact', in another sense 'amend' or 'rectify' and in yet another sense 'admonish' or 'chastise'.

- *Antonyms.* An antonym is a word with the opposite meaning to another of the same language. For example, the word 'big' is opposite to the word 'small', the word 'true' is opposite to the word 'false', and the word 'happy' is opposite to the word 'sad'.

- *Analogy.* An analogy is a relationship between two things where it is necessary to reason the answer from a parallel relationship. This may sound complicated, but it is not. Consider, for example the following question:

HELMET is to PROTECTION as

TIARA is to ADORNMENT, QUEEN, HAIR, ROYALTY, HEAD

The answer is ADORNMENT. Both a helmet and a tiara are worn on the head. However, a helmet is worn for the purpose of protection and a tiara is worn for adornment. Questions in verbal analogy tests typically take the form 'A is to B as C is to ?'; alternatively, they may be presented as:

A : B

C : ?

There is also a third version in which you are asked to identify two words (one from each set of brackets) that form a connection (analogy) when paired with the words in capitals.

- *Classification.* A classification test is generally any test in which the subject is required to sort the material into classes. In the classification test in this section you will be asked to find the odd one out from a group of five words. This may be for a variety of reasons, as in the following examples:

  a. calm, quiet, relaxed, serene, unruffled

  'Quiet' is the odd one out as the rest mean the same thing. However, being quiet does not necessarily mean that you are calm, relaxed, serene or unruffled. You could be extremely upset and agitated but still remain quiet.

  b. thumb, palm, knuckle, knee, finger

  'Knee' is the odd one out as the rest are all part of the hand.

  c. globe, orb, sphere, sceptre, ball

  'Sceptre' is the odd one out as the rest are all circular objects. A sceptre is a ceremonial or emblematic staff.

We all have the ability to classify objects into groups. We all know, for example, that beech, elm, oak and willow are types of trees, so that if we suddenly introduce 'daffodil' into the list it will then be the odd one out because it is a flower. It is this type of thinking that is required to solve the questions in this test, and also some flexibility of thought, in view of the different reasons why one item is the odd one out.

Synonym test A

Instructions: Select just one word in the brackets that is closest in meaning to the word in capitals.

Before commencing the test, work through each of the examples below.

Example 1: ESCAPE (amplify, abscond, defend, concede, allow)

Answer: abscond

Explanation: **escape: to flee**

amplify: to increase in size, volume or significance

abscond: to run away

defend: to protect against a challenge or attack

concede: to yield or make concession

allow: to give permission

ABSCOND is the word closest in meaning to ESCAPE.

Example 2: POSTPONE (move, cancel, alter, defer, stop)

Answer: defer

Explanation: **postpone: defer to a future or later time**

move: change from one place or position to another

cancel: call off or annul something indefinitely

alter: vary or change

defer: put off to a later time

stop: halt or stand still

DEFER is the word closest in meaning to POSTPONE.

You have now 20 minutes in which to solve the following 20 questions.

Q1 ESPOUSAL (illumination, adoption, elimination, abandon, hope)

Answer

Q2 HEARTFELT (cheerful, sensitive, flippant, genuine, sublime)

Answer

Q3 METAPHORICAL (symbolic, philosophical, shambolic, abstract, substantial)

Answer

Q4 WORST (excel, dodge, agonize, change, overpower)

Answer

Q5 MARVEL (hope, subdue, wonder, augment, view)

Answer

Q6 NON-ALIGNED (discreet, chimerical, unclassified, extraneous, impartial)

Answer

Q7 POTENTATE (ruler, effigy, commander, guard, warden)

Answer

Q8 HAUGHTY (tall, jolly, vain, malevolent, gaudy)

Answer

Q9 PSYCHE (thoughts, wisdom, spirit, hopes, fantasy)

Answer

Q10 SPLICE (shard, burst, imbibe, join, gather)

Answer

Q11 VAPID (flavourless, misty, unstable, heterogeneous, small)

Answer

Q12   INEFFECTUAL (still, futile, slow, taboo, inept)

Answer

Q13   ASPERSION (plan, statement, spell, slur, confirmation)

Answer

Q14   PREFATORY (dividend, opening, predilection, hunch, majority)

Answer

Q15   TRENCHANT (deep, tough, hard, vitriolic, cold)

Answer

Q16   FOIBLE (quirk, fortuity, layer, persiflage, zest)

Answer

Q17   WELTER (blow, tangle, weight, target, lump)

Answer

Q18   WREAK (annihilate, encase, jerk, writhe, unleash)

Answer

Q19   CYCLE (rotate, track, sequence, procession, race)

Answer

Q20   SCURRILOUS (wrong, defamatory, urgent, severe, unkind)

Answer

Synonym test B

Instructions: In each question select the two words that are closest in meaning. Before commencing the test, work through each of the examples below.

Example 1: guide, arbiter, colleague, adjudicator, impostor, lawyer

Answer: arbiter, adjudicator

Explanation: guide: to lead or direct

arbiter: someone chosen to judge and decide a disputed issue

colleague: an associate you work with

adjudicator: a person who studies and settles conflicts and disputes

impostor: a person who assumes a character or title not his or her own

lawyer: a professional person authorized to practise law

ARBITER and ADJUDICATOR are the two words closest in meaning.

Example 2: rich, absurd, destitute, different, crucial, affluent

Answer: rich, affluent

Explanation: **rich: of great worth or quality**

absurd: completely devoid of wisdom or good sense

destitute: poverty-stricken

different: not the same

crucial: of extreme importance

affluent: having an abundant supply of money or possessions of value

RICH and AFFLUENT are the two words closest in meaning.

You have now 20 minutes in which to solve the following 20 questions.

Q1   inhibiting, obtrusive, imperceptive, unruly, prying, beset

Answer [   ]

Q2   profuse, reprobate, expert, efficient, bountiful, remarkable

Answer [   ]

Q3   dashing, instinctive, tough, intrepid, liberal, audacious

Answer [   ]

Q4   nosy, obtuse, blunt, awkward, intransigent, casual

Answer [   ]

Q5   range, caper, career, gamut, inception, category

Answer [   ]

Q6   torrid, treasure, sardonic, region, gelid, glacial

Answer [   ]

Q7   outdo, foist, concentrate, impose, frustrate, hoodwink

Answer [   ]

Q8   rift, contrivance, particle, extract, trinket, schism

Answer [   ]

Q9   recycle, rectify, create, adjust, finalize, change

Answer [   ]

Q10   pure, brackish, salty, dark, puerile, clever

Answer [   ]

Q11   assiduous, adroit, authentic, diligent, aggressive, confined

Answer [   ]

Q12   articulate, cognate, forceful, hesitant, similar, intelligent

Answer

Q13   frontage, framework, facet, structure, aspect, foundation

Answer

Q14   pliable, finite, shallow, limited, unsound, boundless

Answer

Q15   celebrate, revere, socialize, vibrate, invert, worship

Answer

Q16   tedium, banality, fascination, operand, inclination, stratagem

Answer

Q17   district, provision, precept, example, rule, precursor

Answer

Q18   delayed, static, damaged, immobile, enervated, irregular

Answer

Q19   luminary, ponderous, hero, highlight, resplendent, dignitary

Answer

Q20   elixir, nosegay, score, reward, posy, scoop

Answer

Antonym test A

Instructions: Select just one word in the brackets that is most opposite in meaning to the word in capitals.

   Before commencing the test, work through each of the examples below.

Example 1: FREQUENT (recurrent, different, rare, never, ancient)

Answer: rare

Explanation: **frequent: happening at short intervals**

recurrent: returning from time to time

different: unlike in nature or quality

rare: recurring only at long intervals

never: not at any time

ancient: very old

RARE is the word most opposite in meaning to FREQUENT.

Example 2: EPILOGUE (speech, postscript, lesson, preface, comment)

Answer: preface

Explanation: **epilogue: a short passage added at the end of a literary work**

speech: communication by word of mouth

postscript: an addition made to a book or composition after the main body of the work

lesson: that which is learnt or taught

preface: an introduction, or series of preliminary remarks

comment: a remark or observation

PREFACE is the word most opposite in meaning to the word EPILOGUE

You have now 20 minutes in which to solve the following 20 questions.

Q1   PROFOUND (unprincipled, intense, thoughtless, deficient, inept)

Answer

Q2   EMANCIPATION (redaction, servitude, redundancy, release, melancholy)

Answer

Q3   ILLOGICAL (proper, correct, coherent, authentic, literate)

Answer

Q4   POSSIBLE (difficult, doubtful, workable, strange, unimaginable)

Answer

Q5   VARIATION (monotony, intensity, apathy, regularity, diversity)

Answer

Q6   RAMBLING (premeditated, prolix, running, direct, feted)

Answer

Q7   SCORN (esteem, love, disagree, reinstate, prefer)

Answer

Q8   ERUDITE (common, prompt, accurate, ignorant, unwilling)

Answer

Q9   UNNECESSARY (prestigious, pressing, contemporary, tangible, dispensable)

Answer

Q10   ROLLICKING (lethargic, slim, morose, sportive, worried)

Answer

Q11 STATIC (chaotic, kinetic, elastic, exotic, dramatic)

Answer [＿＿＿＿＿]

Q12 CAPITULATE (subjugate, relinquish, destroy, succumb, facilitate)

Answer [＿＿＿＿＿]

Q13 RELUCTANT (rigorous, relevant, diligent, inclined, attractive)

Answer [＿＿＿＿＿]

Q14 SPOTLESS (clean, dark, besmirched, extemporize, debased)

Answer [＿＿＿＿＿]

Q15 DWINDLE (ascend, appear, palliate, reap, multiply)

Answer [＿＿＿＿＿]

Q16 REFUTE (approve, confirm, manifest, confute, progress)

Answer [＿＿＿＿＿]

Q17 SCURRY (consider, halt, refine, saunter, spruce)

Answer [＿＿＿＿＿]

Q18 VANGUARD (runner, rear, centre, spearhead, obverse)

Answer [＿＿＿＿＿]

Q19 FICKLE (nonchalant, sad, healthy, invariable, capricious)

Answer [＿＿＿＿＿]

Q20 TALLY (reserve, deduct, differ, pause, hasten)

Answer [＿＿＿＿＿]

Antonym test B

Instructions: In each question select the two words that are most opposite in meaning.

Before commencing the test, work through each of the examples below.

Example 1: register, find, assist, contract, misplace, admire

Answer: find, misplace

Explanation: register: to enrol or enter in a list

find: to discover something

assist: to give help

contract: to make an agreement

misplace: to place something where it cannot be found

admire: to look up to

FIND and MISPLACE are the two words that are most opposite in meaning.

Example 2: crude, snappish, elite, awkward, brittle, polished

Answer: crude, polished

Explanation: **crude: not refined or processed**

snappish: tending to speak irritably

elite: a choice or select group of people or society

awkward: difficult to handle or manage

brittle: having little elasticity; hence easily cracked, fractured or snapped

polished: perfected or made shiny and smooth

CRUDE and POLISHED are the two words that are most opposite in meaning.

You have now 20 minutes in which to solve the following 20 questions.

Q1 sluggish, dominant, menial, regular, subsidiary, inadequate

Answer [   ]

Q2 lively, verbose, laconic, tearful, written, forced

Answer [   ]

Q3 articulate, compelling, fortunate, coincidental, weak, planned

Answer [   ]

Q4 appetizing, stolid, opaque, angry, passionate, hollow

Answer [   ]

Q5 flagrant, clear, cold, winsome, insouciant, subtle

Answer [   ]

Q6 rural, assertive, pastel, droll, vivid, rustic

Answer [   ]

Q7 dormant, stentorian, astute, unperceptive, pugnacious, young

Answer [   ]

Q8 play, please, portray, decide, remonstrate, vex

Answer [   ]

Q9 smart, tasteful, common, tawdry, expensive, new

Answer [   ]

Q10 willing, merry, brusque, affectionate, polite, prostrated

Answer [   ]

Q11 authentic, systematic, indicative, haphazard, classified, compatible

Answer [   ]

Q12 waive, pursue, galvanize, abide, resolve, intercept

Answer

Q13 crafty, complete, fractious, flagrant, affable, peaceful

Answer

Q14 genteel, voracious, sensitive, temperate, soothing, profligate

Answer

Q15 bliss, pestilence, tedium, hardship, succour, heartbreak

Answer

Q16 subjective, willing, obligatory, pedestrian, optional, optimal

Answer

Q17 wisdom, honour, adoration, singularity, fame, ignominy

Answer

Q18 glide, crash, soar, return, plummet, rest

Answer

Q19 decorous, direct, diligent, indigent, temporary, careless

Answer

Q20 respect, daunt, hurry, encourage, impair, bestow

Answer

Analogy test A

Instructions: Before commencing the test, work through each of the examples below.

Example 1: Tree is to Bark as Nut is to: Crunch, Fruit, Kernel, Shell, Acorn

Answer: Shell

Explanation: The outside covering of a tree is the bark, and the outside covering of a nut is the shell.

Example 2: Night is to Evening as Winter is to: Season, Snow, Autumn, Day, Spring

Answer: Autumn

Explanation: Night is immediately preceded by evening, and winter is immediately preceded by autumn.

Example 3: Casino is to Gamble as Synagogue is to: Temple, God, Church, Worship, Kneel

Answer: Worship

Explanation: The main purpose of a casino is to gamble, and the main purpose of a synagogue is to worship.

You have now 20 minutes in which to solve the following 20 questions.

Q1   Why is to Because as Which is to: Therefore, That, Who, How, When

Answer [   ]

Q2   Gather is to Information as Form is to : Assess, Ambition, Impression, Emotion, Ability

Answer [   ]

Q3   Centimetre is to Length as Centigram is to: Area, Capacity, Weight, Velocity, Volume

Answer [   ]

Q4   Inventory is to Stock as Manifest is to: Cargo, Leverage, List, Ship, Goods

Answer [   ]

Q5   Expanse is to Land as Reach is to: Sea, Bridge, Sky, River, Boat

Answer [   ]

Q6   Assegai is to Spear as Mace is to: Weapon, Sword, Catapult, Club, Axe

Answer [   ]

Q7   Ledger is to Accounts as Gazetteer is to: Charts, Places, Records, Lexicon, Journal

Answer [   ]

Q8   Taint is to Tarnish as Foul is to: Sport, Corrupt, Blight, Spill, Pollute

Answer [   ]

Q9   Elucidate is to Expound as Amplify is to: Reason, Explicate, Elaborate, Enquire, Silence

Answer [   ]

Q10   February is to May as August is to: October, Winter, December, June, November

Answer [   ]

Q11   Candle is to Wick as Bulb is to: Light, Filament, Glass, Switch, Electric

Answer [   ]

Q12   University is to Teach as Theatre is to: Music, Actor, Audience, Entertainment, Perform

Answer [   ]

Q13   Gold is to Fifty as Pearl is to: Twenty, Thirty, Thirty-five, Forty, Forty-five

Answer [   ]

Q14 Turret is to Watchtower as Barbican is to: Gatehouse, Dungeon, Rampart, Bastion, Parapet

Answer [   ]

Q15 Astute is to Canny as Prudent is to: Perceptive, Ingenious, Judicious, Clever, Hopeful

Answer [   ]

Q16 Sauté is to Fry as Blanch is to: Roast, Glaze, Bake, Boil, Simmer

Answer [   ]

Q17 Swerve is to Veer as Rotate is to: Sway, Fluctuate, Gyrate, Wobble, Deviate

Answer [   ]

Q18 Skate is to Ice as Dance is to: Partner, Music, Waltz, Floor, Sequence

Answer [   ]

Q19 Hands is to Rotate as Pendulum is to: Time, Swing, Alternate, Movement, Frequency

Answer [   ]

Q20 Cure is to Ward as Punish is to: Confine, Cell, Institution, Beat, Prison

Answer [   ]

Analogy test B

Instructions: In each question you must identify two words (one from each set of brackets) that form a connection (analogy) when paired with the words in capitals.

Before commencing the test, work through each of the examples below.

Example 1: SQUARE (cube, area, number)

CIRCLE (ellipse, sphere, diameter)

Answer: cube, sphere

Explanation: A cube is a three-dimensional square, and a sphere is a three-dimensional circle.

Example 2: PROCLAIM (announce, speak, statute)

ALLEGE (challenge, claim, deny)

Answer: announce, claim

Explanation: When something is proclaimed it is announced; when something is alleged it is claimed.

You have now 20 minutes in which to solve the following 20 questions.

Q1   TUESDAY (Monday, Sunday, Friday)

DECEMBER (March, September, February)

Answer [   ]

Q2   WATER (sea, lake, channel)

LAND (area, isthmus, country)

Answer [   ]

Q3   CIRCLE (radius, globe, sphere)

SQUARE (cube, oblong, area)

Answer [   ]

Q4 NEEDLE (fabric, stitch, thread)
PEN (letter, ink, nib)

Answer

Q5 LEER (anger, lust, disgust)
SCOWL (sorrow, anger, embarrassment)

Answer

Q6 PROCLAIM (announce, explain, predict)
ALLEGE (utter, claim, propound)

Answer

Q7 WOOD (forest, tree, pulp)
COAL (burn, fuel, seam)

Answer

Q8 VENERATE (worship, respect, adore)
EXTOL (homage, compliment, glorify)

Answer

Q9 LATTICE (window, door, joint)
MANSARD (porch, roof, frame)

Answer

Q10 HIGHBROW (stylish, clever, cultivated)
SUAVE (classy, urbane, fashionable)

Answer

Q11 ERGOMANIA (self, work, religion)
PLUTOMANIA (dogs, pleasure, riches)

Answer

Q12 RECLAIM (retrieve, rally, restore)
REVIVE (redeem, recuperate, resuscitate)

Answer

Q13   BOLERO (coat, jacket, dance)
MANTLE (scarf, robe, cloak)

Answer [   ]

Q14   WATT (power, energy, charge)
OHM (current, resistance, inductance)

Answer [   ]

Q15   PETAL (anther, corolla, nectary)
STALK (pedicle, pistil, stamen)

Answer [   ]

Q16   ISOSCELES (pyramid, triangle, hypotenuse)
RECTANGLE (polygon, square, quadrilateral)

Answer [   ]

Q17   POOL (swim, table, water)
TENNIS (ball, racket, court)

Answer [   ]

Q18   ULNA (leg, arm, neck)
METATARSALS (hand, head, foot)

Answer [   ]

Q19   COMPASS (direction, vertex, circles)
PROTRACTOR (lines, angles, geometry)

Answer [   ]

Q20   VIRIDIAN (red, yellow, green)
SIENNA (yellow, brown, red)

Answer [   ]

Comprehension test 1 – word changes

The following test is designed to test verbal skills and ability of comprehension, understanding and appreciation of written text, as well as ability to think quickly under pressure.

In each of the questions you are presented with a sentence that on close scrutiny does not make a great deal of sense. However, by simply changing the position of the number of words indicated, in other words by swapping these words round with each other, it is possible to make the sentence completely comprehensible.

One suggested method of solving these questions is first to read the sentence carefully word for word and as quickly as possible decide in what way it does not make sense, either grammatically or because of word meanings, and then decide what action needs to be taken in order to rewrite the sentence by changing round the number of existing words as indicated in the instructions.

Read the instructions to each question carefully, as these instructions indicate the number of words that require swapping round in each case.

Before commencing the test, study the example below.

Example: Change the position of three words only in the sentence below in order for it to make complete sense.

Pathways in the brain takes the form of electrical communication which run along impulses connecting the various sectors.

Answer: **Communication** in the brain takes the form of electrical **impulses** which run along **pathways** connecting the various sectors.

You have now 90 minutes in which to solve the following 15 questions.

Hyphenated words count as one word only.

Q1   Change the position of four words only in the sentence below in order for it to make complete sense.

Maintain asking for contact face to face it is important to whenever eye something.

_____

Q2   Change the position of five words only in the sentence below in order for it to make complete sense.

In recent series there has been a documentary increase in fly-on-the-wall rapid shows and quiz years.

_____

Q3   Change the position of five words only in the sentence below in order for it to make complete sense.

Many writers keep bedsides at their thoughts and force dreams to arouse from their half-sleep to jot these ideas, themselves and creative notepads down.

_____

Q4   Change the position of four words only in the sentence below in order for it to make complete sense.

In order to fully recognize ourselves we need to understand and be ourselves for what we are, rather than what we would like to know.

_____

Q5   Change the position of four words only in the sentence below in order for it to make complete sense.

At last they came to a road a main way from the little spot, and yet so easily seen that no one would miss it.

_____

Q6   Change the position of eight words only in the sentence below in order for it to make complete sense.

Good acting is desirable much more likely and is better to achieve much impulse generally than judgement on results.

Q7   Change the position of five words only in the sentence below in order for it to make complete sense.

The beauty looking out in all its blue before them, sea as spread as the sky.

Q8   Change the position of four words only in the sentence below in order for it to make complete sense.

Past foundations enable us to build for today and provide the experiences on which we can live for the future.

Q9   Change the position of three words only in the sentence below in order for it to make complete sense.

On his different visit to the zoo the first child reacted with surprise at the number of young creatures that lived in the world.

Q10   Change the position of six words only in the sentence below in order for it to make complete sense.

Technological rate is now taking step at such a latest change that most of us are at least one place behind with the rapid gadgets and innovations.

Q11   Change the position of seven words only in the sentence below in order for it to make complete sense.

When a team does consist of individuals, it be only while these can pull together as a team towards a common goal that the team individuals really is effective.

_____

Q12   Change the position of seven words only in the sentence below in order for it to make complete sense.

He liked assessing friends, widening their circle, finding out more about them and continually observing his people of personalities.

_____

Q13   Change the position of four words only in the sentence below in order for it to make complete sense.

The consommé served a heavy-bodied range of soups from restaurant to full soups such as oxtail.

_____

Q14   Change the position of six words only in the sentence below in order for it to make complete sense.

The long leaves of the stem are rough, rather like a notched saw, and grow in a crown at the tuft of a short dandelion.

_____

Q15   Change the position of seven words only in the sentence below in order for it to make complete sense.

He was creating and saw his wealth, not just as his gateway of life, but as a way to ambitious prominence and career.

_____

Comprehension test 2

As with Comprehension test 1 this test is designed to test verbal skills and ability of comprehension, understanding and appreciation of written text, as well as ability to think quickly under pressure.

Each of the five sentences in the test has had a number of words removed, which have been listed at random below each sentence. You must restore these words correctly into the missing spaces in each sentence in order for it to make complete sense.

Before commencing the test, study the example below.

Example: .... one in three people in Britain have a .... to write a .... , yet only a very small .... of these people .... any further than the .... stage of just .... about it.

Insert the seven missing words correctly into the above sentence.

---

percentage   desire   thinking   novel   approximately   initial   progress

---

Answer: **Approximately** one in three people in Britain have a **desire** to write a **novel**, yet only a very small **percentage** of these people **progress** any further than the **initial** stage of just **thinking** about it.

You have now 45 minutes in which to solve the following five questions.

Q1   For .... people .... more .... , not just over their .... but .... them, means they .... less .... , although this can have the .... if and when it is .... home to them how .... , in .... , they .... control.

Insert the 15 missing words correctly into the above passage.

---

effect   around   fact   many   do   stress   own   feel   having   little
those   lives   control   brought   reverse

Q2   In the .... of .... eels
.... the rivers and then, in ....
.... , ... to the .... , ... they
.... in the ....

Insert the 14 missing words correctly into the above passage.

> bury   numbers   where   spring   return   come   cold   estuaries
> mud   countless   up   themselves   weather   young

Q3   .... has .... been .... , but ....
.... in lifestyle, attitudes and .... that
this change is .... at an ....
.... than ....

Insert the 14 missing words correctly into the above passage.

> greater   always   changes   ever   inevitable   place   technology
> even   change   rate   before   today   mean   taking

Q4   It .... like a very .... at the ....
but .... when ....
.... and .... upon.

Insert the 10 missing words correctly into the above passage.

> through   time   impracticable   seemed   slept   good   thought
> proved   idea   carefully

Q5   In some puzzles .... must be .... , for example that .... at their .... on .... Such puzzles, therefore, can only .... in ....

Insert the 10 missing words correctly into the above passage.

time   certain   destinations   work   made   assumptions   precisely
theory   arrive   trains

Classification

Instructions: This test consists of 20 questions designed to test your ability in collecting together objects or ideas that belong to a set or have some common attribute.

In each question select just one word, from the choice of five words provided, that is the odd one out.

Before commencing the test, work through each of the examples below.

Example 1: purchaser, vendor, buyer, customer, client

Answer: vendor

Explanation: A vendor is a seller. The rest are all buyers or potential buyers.

Example 2: abode, dwelling, domicile, residence, street

Answer: street

Explanation: 'Street' is the odd one out as the rest are specific names for places where people live. A street may contain many types of buildings as well as gardens, trees, road surfaces etc.

You have now 30 minutes in which to solve the following 20 questions.

Q1   idiom, nonsense, locution, motto, utterance

Answer [   ]

Q2   elaborate, expound, enlarge, extemporize, expatiate

Answer [   ]

Q3   period, age, epoch, cosmos, era

Answer [   ]

Q4   reflective, serene, meditative, contemplative, pensive

Answer [   ]

Q5   defile, deprave, foul, pollute, sully

Answer [   ]

Q6   piccolo, violin, trombone, bassoon, oboe

Answer [   ]

Q7   scalpel, baroscope, sextant, pedometer, callipers

Answer [   ]

Q8   crevice, cranny, fissure, chasm, cleft

Answer [   ]

Q9   plight, quandary, straits, snag, predicament

Answer [   ]

Q10   hindmost, ultimate, end, primary, final

Answer [   ]

Q11   interim, provisionary, temporary, perennial, transitional

Answer [   ]

Q12   ninety degrees, fifteen minutes, thirteen weeks, thirty seconds, twenty-five per cent

Answer [   ]

Q13   sunder, mollify, macerate, mute, palliate

Answer [   ]

Q14   cornea, lens, lobe, pupil, iris

Answer [   ]

Q15   red, blue, indigo, brown, orange

Answer [   ]

Q16   chair, sofa, pew, table, settee

Answer [   ]

Q17   semibreve, treble, minim, quaver, crotchet

Answer [   ]

Q18   scoff, scold, jeer, mock, deride

Answer [   ]

Q19   exacting, inconceivable, arduous, formidable, onerous

Answer [   ]

Q20   cancel, amend, repeal, rescind, revoke

Answer [   ]

Letter sequences

In any sequence test, whether it be visual, numerical or, as in the case of this test, letter sequences, it is necessary first to identify a pattern that is occurring and after establishing such a pattern decide what should come next in the sequence.

The questions are presented in a number of different ways: as a simple one-line letter sequence, as groups of letters or as letters arranged in shapes such as a square matrix or pyramid.

The test, therefore, also tests ability to adapt to various styles of question and flexibility of mind in quickly analysing data presented and exploring various options and possibilities in identifying correctly the patterns that are occurring.

The instructions to each question should be read carefully before the question is attempted.

Before commencing the test, work through each of the examples below.

Example 1: A   C   E   G   I   ?

What letter comes next?

Answer: K

Explanation: Skip one letter in the alphabet each time: AbCdEfGhIjK

Example 2: A   D   G   J   M   ?

What letter comes next?

Answer: P

Explanation: Skip two letters of the alphabet each time:
AbcDefGhiJklMnoP

Example 3:

A   C   E

D   F   H

G   I   ?

What letter should replace the question mark?

Answer: K

Explanation: Looking at each line across skip one letter, for example: AbCdE

Looking at each line down skip two letters, for example: AbcDefG

You have now 20 minutes in which to solve the following 10 questions.

Q1   GMS is to HLT as KTW is to: JUV, LSX, LUX, JSV, LSV.

Answer [   ]

Q2   What letter should replace the question mark?

    E   G   I

    H   J   L

    K   M   ?

Answer [   ]

Q3   Which two letters come next?

    A   C   F   H   K   M   ?   ?

Answer [   ]

Q4   What letters should replace the question marks?

    A

    CD

    ???

    JKLM

    OPQRS

Answer [   ]

Q5

A	C	F	H
D	F		K
F	H	K	
I	K	N	

Which is the missing section?

H	
	L
	P

A

I	
	L
	O

B

I	
	M
	P

C

H	
	M
	O

D

Answer

Q6   AZ   CX   FU   JQ   ??

What letters come next?

Answer

Q7   ABDC   BCED   CDFE   DEGF   ????

What letters come next?

Answer

Q8   A   G   L   P   ?

What letter comes next?

Answer

Q9   ABDEHIMN??

Which two letters come next?

Answer

Q10   MN   LO   JQ   GT   ??

Which two letters come next?

Answer

Multidiscipline verbal test

This test is a miscellaneous selection of 20 verbal questions designed to measure language use or comprehension, and your ability to adapt to different types of question.

The test brings together many of the elements contained in the previous tests in this section, in addition to which there are several questions involving the use of grammar and punctuation.

Instructions: You have 50 minutes in which to solve the 20 questions.

You should read the instructions to each question carefully before it is attempted.

Q1   Which word in brackets is closest in meaning to the word in capitals?

HIATUS (period, plateau, gap, climax, barrier)

Answer [   ]

Q2   The defendant sought .... from his .... whether he should plead guilty or not guilty.

Place the correct words into the above sentence from the choice below:

advise, advice

council, counsel

Answer [   ]

Q3   The .... professor warned about the .... dangers of global warming.

Select the two correct words from the choice below and place them in the correct position to complete the above sentence correctly.

immanent, eminent, imminent

Answer [   ]

Q4   The salespeople, who met their targets, were rewarded with a bonus.

Amend the punctuation in the above sentence if, or where, necessary in order to convey the meaning that only salespeople who met their targets were rewarded with a bonus.

Answer [   ]

Q5   Which word in brackets is most opposite in meaning to the word in capitals?

LUXURY (indulgence, sin, austerity, difficulty, mendacity)

Answer [   ]

Q6   The .... strike, which had the .... of .... up the whole sky, was followed by an angry rumble of thunder.

Place three of the words below into their correct position in the sentence above.

| lightening   effect   lightning   affect |

Answer [   ]

Q7   It was important that the correct .... of items were chosen from the .... of goods on offer.

Place the words below into their correct position in the above sentence.

| amount   number |

Answer [   ]

Q8   The .... workers who left Great Britain for new jobs in Germany were .... employed in the mining industry in the North-East of England.

Place two of the four words below into their correct position in the above sentence.

| immigrant   formally   formerly   emigrant |

Answer [   ]

Q9   Which two words are closest in meaning?

nativity, naturalism, nudism, realism, adoption, style

Answer [   ]

Q10   Which one of the sentences below is grammatically correct?

a.   'Its amazing', said the lady, 'to see how quickly my little dog is able to bury its bone in the garden'.

b.   'It's amazing', said the lady, 'to see how quickly my little dog is able to bury its bone in the garden'.

c.   'It's amazing', said the lady, 'to see how quickly my little dog is able to bury it's bone in the garden'.

d.   'It's amazing,' said the lady, 'to see how quickly my little dog is able to bury its bone in the garden'.

e.   'It's amazing,' said the lady, 'to see how quickly my little dog is able to bury it's bone in the garden'.

Answer [   ]

Q11   Statute is to Ordinance as Mandate is to: Directive, Proclamation, Request, Oath, Monition.

Answer [   ]

Q12   Identify two words (one from each set of brackets) that form a connection (analogy) when paired with the words in capitals.

LEARN (school, taught, gain)

TEACH (educate, impart, college)

Answer [   ]

Q13   Identify two words (one from each set of brackets) that form a connection (analogy) when paired with the words in capitals.

DEFECTIVE (short, goods, faulty)

DEFICIENT (faulty, wanting, inconclusive)

Answer [   ]

Q14   Which is the odd one out?

dale, knoll, rift, glen, gulch

Answer [   ]

Q15 Which is the odd one out?

belated, overdue, late, dilatory, rescinded

Answer [   ]

Q16 Which word in brackets is closest in meaning to the word in capitals?

PIED (tiny, spirited, pointed, dappled, dull)

Answer [   ]

Q17 Which two words are closest in meaning?

prosperous, palpable, manifest, trembling, imposing, cautious

Answer [   ]

Q18 Which two words are most opposite in meaning?

pathetic, tedious, vulgar, willing, forceful, enthralling

Answer [   ]

Q19 Which is the odd one out?

surplus, expanse, glut, plethora, surfeit

Answer [   ]

Q20 Identify two words (one from each set of brackets) that form a connection (analogy) when paired with the words in capitals.

WATERMARK (sign, identification, paper)

HALLMARK (purity, gold, stamp)

Answer [   ]

Lexical ability test

This test consists of three different styles of questions, each designed to test your powers of vocabulary in a different way.

Instructions:

Questions 1–10
In this part of the test you are given the first part of a word or phrase and you have to find the second part. This second part then becomes the first part of the second word or phrase.

For example: back (   ) breaking. The word *ground* would then complete the word back*ground*, and the word *ground* would also commence the phrase *ground*-breaking.

Questions 11–20
This set of questions is designed to test the ability to find quickly alternative meanings of words. In each case you are looking for a word having the same meanings as the two definitions provided.

For example: travelling entertainment (   ) free from discrimination. The word you are looking for is *fair*, which means the same as the definition on the left-hand side of the brackets in one sense and the same as the definition on the right-hand side in another sense.

Questions 21–30
This set of questions is designed to test knowledge of word meanings and spelling ability by identifying letter patterns from which to construct a nine-letter word with the aid of the definition provided. In each case you are given nine three-letter bits and must identify the correct three three-letter bits in order to produce the nine-letter word.

For example, the word *haphazard* consists of the three three-letter bits, *hap*, *haz*, *ard*.

Before commencing the test, work through each of the examples below.

Example 1 (questions 1–10): trigger (   ) event

Answer: happy

Explanation: to produce the hyphenated phrase 'trigger-happy' and the two-word phrase 'happy event'

Example 2 (questions 1–10): man (   ) red

Answer: kind

Explanation: to produce the words 'mankind' and 'kindred'

Example 3 (questions 11–20): financial institution (   ) side of a river

Answer: bank

Example 4 (questions 21–30): something that holds things:

TAI   UPT   PIN   CON   ERG   ERT   ANY   NER   PAT

Answer: container (CON–TAI–NER)

You have now 90 minutes in which to solve the following 30 questions.

    As each section is approximately the same level of difficulty it is suggested that you pace yourself so that you spend approximately 30 minutes on each group of 10 questions.

Questions 1–10
Insert a word in the brackets that will complete a word or phrase when placed behind the word on the left, and another word or phrase when placed in front of the word on the right.

Q1   royal (   ) print

Answer [   ]

Q2   light (   ) long

Answer [   ]

Q3   new (   ) beam

Answer [   ]

Q4   fire (   ) new

Answer [   ]

Q5   high (   ) blank

Answer [   ]

Q6   mill (   ) wall

Answer [   ]

Q7   loss (   ) ship

Answer [   ]

Q8   river (   ) note

Answer [   ]

Q9   play (   ) chant

Answer [   ]

Q10   quick (   ) son

Answer [   ]

Questions 11–20

Place a word in the brackets that means the same as the definitions either side of the brackets.

Q11   one circuit of a running track (   ) wash against

Answer [   ]

Q12   hurl or throw (   ) dark viscid substance   *Answer* [   ]

Q13   growl viciously (   ) a knot in wood   *Answer* [   ]

Q14   a line of hurdles (   ) the act of running away   Answer [   ]

Q15   stick or metal bar (   ) financial interest   *Answer* [   ]

Q16   medium of illumination (   ) underweight   *Answer* [   ]

Q17   knitting stitch (   ) swirling movement of water   *Answer* [   ]

Q18   relaxation (   ) remainder   *Answer* [   ]

Q19   cash register (   ) plough   *Answer* [   ]

Q20   hurriedly (   ) abstain from eating   *Answer* [   ]

Questions 21–30

In each of the following combine three of the three-letter bits to form a nine-letter word with the aid of the clue provided.

Q21   A long and complicated procedure

UAL   TIM   MAR   PAR   RIG   ANT   OLE   ARE   ONE

Answer [   ]

Q22   Resembling a force of nature

TAL   EAR   ATE   ELE   CAN   PIN   MAR   MEN   OUR

Answer [   ]

Q23 Portion of land

AGE   INS   TED   OUP   ULA   ART   PEN   END   ORA

Answer _____

Q24 Supple

OND   HES   IGA   IGH   LIT   OME   ITE   SPR   LIS

Answer _____

Q25 Pertaining to the ear

ONO   LAR   ICU   ERE   AUR   AUD   ILA   TER   LOT

Answer _____

Q26 Ceramic ware

CEL   ICA   POR   AUD   AIN   INE   MOR   DAT   TER

Answer _____

Q27 The final point in a process

TRA   ULT   OUR   NCE   TOR   RES   SER   ANT   IDU

Answer _____

Q28 Not conforming to approved standards

IMI   THI   IED   AIL   CAL   UNE   ARN   HED   LED

Answer _____

Q29 To glitter in flashes

IVE   USC   INE   ACE   ATE   RIG   TIS   SUM   COR

Answer _____

Q30 Measuring instrument

TOR   IME   ERA   ALT   POR   AVA   ERN   TER   LUT

Answer _____

CHAPTER 2

Numerical aptitude

Mathematical intelligence tests generally explore your ability to reason and to perform basic arithmetic functions. Sometimes flexibility of thought and lateral thinking processes are also necessary in order to solve the problems that are presented. Numerical aptitude helps you to understand geometric shapes and manipulate equations. It is also a strong indicator of general intelligence, as many everyday tasks require arithmetical operations or thought processes even though numbers may not be involved.

Numerical questions are widely used in IQ testing and, as numbers are international, numerical tests are regarded as being culture-fair, or culture-free, and designed to be free of any particular cultural bias so that no advantage is derived by individuals of one culture relative to those of another.

These tests, therefore, eliminate language factors or other skills that may be closely tied to another culture, and are frequently designed to test powers of logic and ability to deal with problems in a structured and analytical way. Individual tests include mental arithmetic, number sequences and logical reasoning, all designed to test a person's aptitude or ability at mathematical calculation, identifying number patterns and reasoning with numbers.

Such tests enable employers to test the numerical aptitude of candidates and to determine their proficiency and the extent of their knowledge when dealing with numbers, and their ability to apply this knowledge to the solving of mathematical problems.

When preparing for numerical ability tests it will be useful to bear in mind the following points:

- The main function of a numerical ability test is to determine how well a person can reason with numbers. The test is likely to require straightforward mathematical calculation: division, subtraction, multiplication or addition.

- Sometimes you may also be presented with problems that require mathematical calculations to solve them. In this case, although such questions may at first glance appear complex or confusing, the actual mathematics involved may be quite simple, and you are being assessed on your ability to apply this knowledge quickly and accurately in order to find the most effective way of arriving at the correct solution.

- In a numerical sequence test first identify a pattern that is occurring in the sequence, and after establishing such a pattern decide what should come next in the sequence. It is advisable to look for simple sequences first. For example, are the numbers progressively increasing or decreasing? Is there a sequence of numbers that increase and then decrease in turn. After eliminating seemingly simple sequences, look for other possibilities. For example, are there two alternate, interwoven sequences? Is an even more complex sequence occurring such as multiply by 1, add 2, multiply by 3, add 4 etc? If you are asked to provide the next two numbers in a sequence, this may be a clue to the fact that there are two separate but interwoven sequences.

- Read each question very carefully. Sometimes if you misread, or even fail to read, just one word in the question, this may mean the difference between a correct answer and an incorrect answer – so concentrate very hard and ensure you not only follow the test instructions but fully understand each question within the test before you attempt it.

- Brush up on basic mathematical functions and principles, especially if it is some time since you last used them. Examples are given on the next page.

Addition

The result of adding together two or more numbers is referred to as the sum. Memorize the simplest combinations of sums. This may seem over-simple or even too basic. However, if you ensure such information is committed to memory, so that it can be instantly recalled, thinking time may be considerably reduced, and anything that helps to keep you one step ahead in the game is likely to improve your overall test results.

The following table represents the sums of any two digits from 1 to 9 and 11:

	1	2	3	4	5	6	7	8	9	11
1	2	3	4	5	6	7	8	9	10	12
2	3	4	5	6	7	8	9	10	11	13
3	4	5	6	7	8	9	10	11	12	14
4	5	6	7	8	9	10	11	12	13	15
5	6	7	8	9	10	11	12	13	14	16
6	7	8	9	10	11	12	13	14	15	17
7	8	9	10	11	12	13	14	15	16	18
8	9	10	11	12	13	14	15	16	17	19
9	10	11	12	13	14	15	16	17	18	20
11	12	13	14	15	16	17	18	19	20	22

Multiplication

The result of multiplying two or more numbers together is referred to as the product. Although the arithmetic operation of multiplication is most commonly indicated by the times sign ($\times$), sometimes a dot or star is used to indicate the multiplication of two or more numbers, and in some cases parentheses are used. For example, 5×9, $5 \cdot 9$, $5 * 9$ and $(5)(9)$ all indicate the product of 5 times 9.

It is of great advantage, especially in tests that do not allow the use of calculating machines, to memorize the basic multiples of integers from 1 to 12.

The table below shows the products of all the numbers from 1 to 12 (omitting 1 and 10) and 75:

	2	3	4	5	6	7	8	9	11	12	75
2	4	6	8	10	12	14	16	18	22	24	150
3	6	9	12	15	18	21	24	27	33	36	225
4	8	12	16	20	24	28	32	36	44	48	300
5	10	15	20	25	30	35	40	45	55	60	375
6	12	18	24	30	36	42	48	54	66	72	450
7	14	21	28	35	42	49	56	63	77	84	525
8	16	24	32	40	48	56	64	72	88	96	600
9	18	27	36	45	54	63	72	81	99	108	675
11	22	33	44	55	66	77	88	99	121	132	825
12	24	36	48	60	72	84	96	108	132	144	900
75	150	225	300	375	450	525	600	675	825	900	5625

Some other basic mathematical principles

- Two negative numbers, for example –1, –2, multiplied together always produce a positive number

- A negative number multiplied by a positive number will produce a negative number.

- When dividing fractions, for example $\frac{1}{2} \div \frac{1}{4}$, always reverse the second fraction and multiply, thus $\frac{1}{2} \div \frac{1}{4}$ becomes $\frac{1}{2} \times \frac{4}{1} = \frac{4}{2} = 2$

  The answer, in this case, is referred to as the quotient, which is the result obtained from division.

- Quick checks for divisibility:

  - Divide by 2:
    A number is always divisible by 2 exactly if the last digit is divisible by 2.

  - Divide by 3 (or 9):
    If the sum of the digits of a number is divisible by 3, then that number or any combination of the same digits also divides exactly by 3, as in the case of the

number 3912, whose digits total 15, which divides by 3 exactly. Similarly, the digits 497286 total 36, which divides by 9, so any combination of these digits also divides exactly by 9.

- Divide by 4:
  If the last two digits of any number are divisible by 4, then the number itself is also divisible by 4, for example 712688 is divisible by 4 exactly because 88 is divisible by 4.

- Divide by 5:
  A number is divisible by 5 exactly if it ends in 0 or 5.

- Divide by 6:
  A number is divisible by 6 exactly if it is divisible by 2 and 3.
  Any even number divisible by 3 is also divisible by 6, for example 6, 12, 18, 24 etc.

- Divide by 10:
  A number is only divisible by 10 exactly when it ends in 0.
  To divide a decimal by 10, move the decimal point back one place, for example $123.45 \div 10 = 12.345$. Similarly when dividing by 100 move the decimal point back two places, so $123.45 \div 100 = 1.2345$.

- Divide by 12:
  Any number is divisible by 12 exactly if it is divisible by 3 and 4 exactly.

● Two or more even numbers multiplied together always produce an even number.

● Two or more odd numbers multiplied together always produce an odd number.

● Any string of numbers multiplied together that includes at least one even number always produces an even number.

● Square numbers: A square number is the result of a number being multiplied by itself. For example 4×4 (16) is written 4^2 and called 4 squared. The first few square numbers (below 1000) are: 1, 4, 9, 16, 25, 36, 49, 64, 81, 100, 121, 144, 169, 196, 225, 256, 289, 324, 361, 400, 441, 484, 529, 576, 625, 676, 729, 784, 841, 900, 961.

● Cube numbers: A cube number is the result of a number multiplied by itself twice, for example $2 \times 2 \times 2$ (8) is written 2^3 and is called 2 cubed. The first few cube numbers (below 1000) are: 1, 8, 27, 64, 125, 216, 343, 512, 729.

- To obtain the average of a set of numbers, total up the numbers and divide the result by how many numbers there are in the set. For example, the average of the seven numbers 3, 8, 6, 17, 82, 3 and 14 is the total of these numbers, 133, divided by 7 (because there are seven numbers) = 19.

- When anything is divided or multiplied by zero the answer is always zero.

- Prime numbers: any number greater than 1 that has no factors (numbers that divide into it without remainder) other than 1 and itself; 1 is not considered to be a prime number. The first few prime numbers (up to 100) are: 2, 3, 5, 7, 11, 13, 17, 19, 23, 29, 31, 37, 41, 43, 47, 53, 59, 61, 67, 71, 73, 79, 83, 89, 97.

Numerical sequence test

This test is designed to test your numerical dexterity and quickness of thought. In a numerical sequence test it is necessary to identify a pattern that is occurring in the sequence. The numbers in the sequence may be progressing, or they may be decreasing, and in some cases they may be both progressing and decreasing within the sequence. It is up to you to determine how this is occurring and either to continue the sequence or to provide a missing number within the sequence.

For example in the following sequence:

1, 9, 17, 25, 33, ?

the missing number is 41, as the numbers in the sequence are increasing by 8 each time.

However, in the more complex sequence:

100, 99, 97, 96, 94, 93, ?

the missing number is 91, as the numbers in the sequence are decreasing by 1, then 2, alternately.

Instructions: Fill in the missing number(s) indicated by the question mark in each sequence.

The use of a calculating machine is not permitted in this test.

Before commencing the test, work through each of the examples below.

Example 1: 0, 3, ?, 9, 12, 15, 18

Answer: 6

Explanation: Add 3 each time.

Example 2: 0, 3, ?, 12, 18, 25, 33

Answer: 7

Explanation: The amount added on is 1 more each time, ie 3, 4, 5, 6, 7, 8.

Example 3: 0, 100, 3, 97, 6, 94, 9, 91, 12, ?, ?

Answer: 88, 15

Explanation: There are two alternate and interwoven sequences. The first starts at 0 and adds 3 each time: 0, 3, 6, 9, 12, **15**. The second starts at 100 and deducts 3 each time: 100, 97, 94, 91, **88**.

You have now 20 minutes in which to solve the following 20 questions.

Q1   16, 32, 48, 64, 80, 96, ?

Answer [   ]

Q2   2.7, 5.4, 8.1, 10.8, ?

Answer [   ]

Q3   1, 6, 16, 31, 51, ?

Answer [   ]

Q4   100, 110, 121, 133.1, ?

Answer [   ]

Q5   100, 91, 85, 76, 70, ?

Answer [   ]

Q6   2½, 4¼, 6, 7¾, ?

Answer [   ]

Q7   1, 4, 9, 16, 25, 36, ?, 64

Answer [   ]

Q8   100, 99, 97, 94, 90, 85, ?, 72

Answer [   ]

Q9   5, 5, 10, 30, 30, 60, 180, 180, ?

Answer [   ]

Q10   100, 90¼, 80½, 70¾, ?

Answer [   ]

Q11   1, 8, 22, 43, 71, ?

Answer [   ]

Q12   1, 100, 8, 91, 15, 82, 22, 73, ?, ?

Answer [   ]

Q13   1, 2, 6, 12, 36, 72, ?

Answer [   ]

Q14   56, 112, 224, 448, 896, ?

Answer [   ]

Q15   1, 1, 4, 7, 7, 13, 10, 19, 13, 25, ?, ?

Answer [   ]

Q16   100, 93.25, 86.5, 79.75, 73, ?

Answer [   ]

Q17   100, 1, 97.5, 8.5, 95, 16, 92.5, 23.5, 90, ?, ?

Answer [   ]

Q18   1, 1, 3, –2, 5, –5, 7, –8, 9, –11, 11, ?, ?

Answer [   ]

Q19   1, 4, 12, 15, 45, 48, ?

Answer [   ]

Q20   1000, 736, 472, 208, ?

Answer [   ]

Mathematical calculation test

This test is designed to test basic arithmetic skills of addition, subtraction, multiplication and division, as well as the ability to work quickly and accurately under pressure.

Instructions: In each question a mathematical sum (equation) is contained within a number of boxes. In each case a number is missing from one of the boxes and you have to select the correct box from the options given in order to complete the equation correctly.

The use of a calculating machine is not permitted in this test.

Before commencing the test, work through each of the examples below.

Example 1:

Which is the missing box?

Answer: D

Explanation: 5 + 3 (8) = 15 − 7 (8)

Example 2:

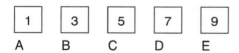

Which is the missing box?

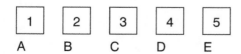

Answer: C

Explanation: 23 × 2 (46) = 138 ÷ 3 (46)

You have now 20 minutes in which to solve the following 20 questions.

Q1

Which is the missing box?

66	59	56	69	57
A	B	C	D	E

Answer [   ]

Q2

84 − [ ] = 35

Which is the missing box?

41	59	51	39	49
A	B	C	D	E

Answer [   ]

Q3

8 × [ ] = 76

Which is the missing box?

9.5	9.25	9	8.5	12
A	B	C	D	E

Answer [   ]

Q4

135 ÷ [ ] = 4.5

Which is the missing box?

25	27.5	30	35	37.5
A	B	C	D	E

Answer [   ]

Q5

| 7 | × | | = | 28 | × | 3 |

Which is the missing box?

| 8 | 12 | 9 | 16 | 14 |
| A | B | C | D | E |

Answer

Q6

| 9 | × | 8 | = | | + | 33 |

Which is the missing box?

| 29 | 35 | 37 | 39 | 49 |
| A | B | C | D | E |

Answer

Q7

| 255 | ÷ | | = | 315 | ÷ | 21 |

Which is the missing box?

| 15 | 16 | 17 | 18 | 19 |
| A | B | C | D | E |

Answer

Q8

| 16 | × | | = | 30 | × | 4 |

Which is the missing box?

| 7.5 | 6 | 6.5 | 8 | 5 |
| A | B | C | D | E |

Answer

Q9

| 6 | × | 9 | × | 3 | = | 8 | × | |

Which is the missing box?

| 20.25 | 20 | 18 | 21.5 | 18.5 |
| A | B | C | D | E |

Answer [ ]

Q10

| 17 | + | 15 | − | 8 | = | | ÷ | 3 |

Which is the missing box?

| 69 | 72 | 75 | 78 | 84 |
| A | B | C | D | E |

Answer [ ]

Q11

| 1 | 0 | 4 | 4 | ÷ | | 7 | = | 1 | 2 |

Which is the missing box?

| 5 | 6 | 7 | 8 | 9 |
| A | B | C | D | E |

Answer [ ]

Q12

| | × | 5 | = | 4 | 7 |

Which is the missing box?

| 8.2 | 8.4 | 9.2 | 9.4 | 9.8 |
| A | B | C | D | E |

Answer [ ]

Q13

| 9 | 1 | ÷ | 1 | | = | 7 |

Which is the missing box?

| 1 | 2 | 3 | 7 | 9 |
| A | B | C | D | E |

Answer

Q14

| 7 | | + | 2 | 9 | = | 3 | 6 | × | 3 |

Which is the missing box?

| 5 | 9 | 3 | 8 | 7 |
| A | B | C | D | E |

Answer

Q15

| 11 | × | | = | 2 | 3 | 1 | ÷ | 4 |

Which is the missing box?

| 4.25 | 4.5 | 4.75 | 5.25 | 5.75 |
| A | B | C | D | E |

Answer

Q16

| 3 | 2 | × | 8 | = | 7 | | 8 | ÷ | 3 |

Which is the missing box?

| 2 | 4 | 6 | 8 | 0 |
| A | B | C | D | E |

Answer

Q17

| 2 | 4 | 7 | ÷ | | = | 2 | 6 |

Which is the missing box?

| 9.5 | 8 | 6.5 | 7.5 | 7 |
| A | B | C | D | E |

Answer [ ]

Q18

| 7 | 2 | ÷ | 1 | 2 | = | 3 | | ÷ | 5.5 |

Which is the missing box?

| 0 | 1 | 2 | 3 | 4 |
| A | B | C | D | E |

Answer [ ]

Q19

| 4 | | − | 1 | 9 | = | 2 | 9 |

Which is the missing box?

| 4 | 5 | 6 | 7 | 8 |
| A | B | C | D | E |

Answer [ ]

Q20

| 1 | 4 | × | 2 | 8 | = | 3 | | 2 |

Which is the missing box?

| 0 | 9 | 7 | 5 | 1 |
| A | B | C | D | E |

Answer [ ]

Mental arithmetic test

This test is designed to test your powers of mental arithmetic and is a speed test of 30 questions, which gradually increase in difficulty as the test progresses.

 You should work quickly and calmly and try to think at all times of the quickest and most efficient way of tackling the questions.

Instructions: The use of a calculator is not permitted in this test and only the answer should be committed to paper, the object of the test being that all the working out is done in your head.

 Before commencing the test, work through each of the examples below.

Example 1: What is 18 multiplied by 3 and then divided by 9?

Answer: 6: 18 × 3 = 54 and 54 ÷ 9 = 6

Suggested short cut: 18 ÷ 9 = 2 and 2 × 3 = 6

This saves having to multiply 18 by 3 and then dividing the answer by 9.

Example 2: What is 40% of 110?

Answer: 44

Suggested short cut: 10% of 110 = 11 (110 less the zero); then 11 × 4 = 44

Example 3: What is 598 plus 271?

Answer: 869

Suggested short cut: add 271 to 600 and deduct 2; alternatively add 269 to 600

You have now 45 minutes in which to solve the following 30 questions.

Q1   What is 9 multiplied by 8?

 Answer [＿＿＿＿＿＿]

Q2   What is 59 plus 14?

 Answer [＿＿＿＿＿＿]

Q3 What is 89 minus 22?

Answer [ ]

Q4 What is 14 multiplied by 7?

Answer [ ]

Q5 What is 18 plus 7 plus 9?

Answer [ ]

Q6 What is 60% of 120?

Answer [ ]

Q7 What is 16 multiplied by 3 and then divided by 2?

Answer [ ]

Q8 What is 96 divided by 6?

Answer [ ]

Q9 What is 17 + 19 + 4 + 7?

Answer [ ]

Q10 What is 75 multiplied by 9?

Answer [ ]

Q11 What is 277 minus 86?

Answer [ ]

Q12 What is 45% of 150?

Answer [ ]

Q13 What is ½ + ¾ + ¾?

Answer [ ]

Q14   What is 5/6 of 336?

Answer

Q15   Multiply 15 by 8 and add 12.

Answer

Q16   What is 96 less 27?

Answer

Q17   What is 583 plus 28?

Answer

Q18   What is 966 less 492?

Answer

Q19   What is 28 multiplied by 12?

Answer

Q20   What is 2842 divided by 14?

Answer

Q21   What is ¾ of 428?

Answer

Q22   What is 65% of 260?

Answer

Q23   What is 482 plus 69 plus 125?

Answer

Q24   What is 79 multiplied by 11?

Answer

Q25   What is 10652 less 723?

                                        Answer [   ]

Q26   What is 884 divided by 17?

                                        Answer [   ]

Q27   What is 336 plus 194 and then divided by 2?

                                        Answer [   ]

Q28   What is 2/5 of 585?

                                        Answer [   ]

Q29   What is 70% of 290 plus 40% of 180?

                                        Answer [   ]

Q30   What is 7/9 of 1278?

                                        Answer [   ]

General numerical aptitude test

This test brings together a variety of different types of questions designed to test powers of calculation and computation and logical reasoning, the ability to work quickly and accurately with numbers and ability to adapt to different types of question.

Instructions: You should read the instructions to each question carefully before it is attempted.

The use of a calculator is not permitted in this test.

Before commencing the test, work through each of the examples below.

Example 1: 7   5   6   3   2   1

What is the difference between the sum of the six numbers above and the average of the six numbers above?

Answer: 20

Explanation: Sum (or total) is $7 + 5 + 6 + 3 + 2 + 1 = 24$.

Average (sum divided by how many numbers) is $24 \div 6 = 4$.

The difference is, therefore, $24 - 4 = 20$.

Example 2 (involving a degree of lateral thinking):

2	3
4	6

1	2
2	4

1	3
2	?

What number should replace the question mark?

Answer: 6

Explanation: In each square, the number formed by the two digits at the top is half the number formed by the two digits at the bottom. Thus, 23 is half of 46, 12 is half of 24 and 13 is half of 26. The missing number is, therefore, 6.

You have now 60 minutes in which to solve the following 15 questions.

Q1

20	34	18	30	25
10	6	24	3	12
9	17	13	8	19
14	11	21	7	16
1	4	15	2	5

Looking at straight lines of numbers, either horizontally, vertically or diagonally, what number is two places away from itself plus 4, three places away from itself divided by 3, two places away from itself multiplied by 2 and three places away from itself less 1?

Answer

Q2   Find five consecutive numbers below that total 24.

7 2 9 3 4 5 6 9 1 3 7 3 9 1 5 4 6 9 2 5

Answer

Q3   Stanley has £30.00 more than Oliver, but then Oliver wins some money on a racehorse and trebles his money, which means that he now has £20.00 more than the original amount of money that the two men had between them. How much money did Stanley and Oliver have between them before Oliver's win?

Answer

Q4

17	27	22	25
34	14	7	31
42	15	4	18
2	16	41	12

Identify a number in the grid that meets the two following simple rules:

a. It is not in any line across that contains a square number, for example 9 (3 × 3) is a square number.

b. It is not in any line down that contains a prime number (a prime number is any number above 1 that is divisible only by itself and 1).

Answer [   ]

Q5 How many minutes is it before 12 noon if one hour ago it was five times as many minutes past 9 am?

Answer [   ]

Q6 3 9 3 5 3 8 7 1 6

What is the difference between the average of the numbers above and the second-highest odd number?

Answer [   ]

Q7 1, 1, 2, 4, 7, 11, ?, 22, 29, 37

What number should replace the question mark?

Answer [   ]

Q8

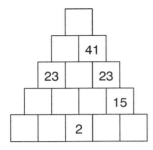

Each number in the pyramid is the sum of the two numbers immediately below it. Fill in the pyramid with the missing numbers.

Q9   LEFT   RIGHT

24	3	32	23	52
37	15	18	20	84
11	16	9	48	7
12	19	8	13	1
54	22	17	96	68

18	14	24	13	9
7	25	1	12	32
15	8	36	20	5
3	17	2	28	23
18	26	11	19	16

Multiply the third-highest odd number in the left-hand grid with the third-lowest even number in the right-hand grid.

Answer [   ]

Q10   5, 5, 7, 6, 11, 9, 19, 14, 35, ?, ?

Which two numbers continue the above sequence?

Answer [   ]

Q11   My watch was correct at midnight, after which it began to lose 6 minutes per hour, until 5 hours ago it stopped completely. It now shows the time as 3.36. What is the correct time now?

Answer [   ]

Q12 Assuming A = 3, B = 4, C = 6, D = 7, E = 8, what mathematical sign should replace the question mark?

(B × E) ? D = (C × A) + (D × A)

Answer [   ]

Questions 13–15
The following three questions are specifically designed to test your powers of logic, and your ability to work with numbers and to identify relationships between numbers.

Q13

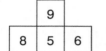

What number should replace the question mark?

Answer [   ]

Q14

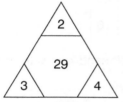 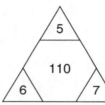 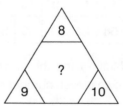

What number should replace the question mark?

Answer [   ]

Q15

What number should replace the question mark?

Answer [   ]

Advanced number diagrams test – calculation and logic

This exercise is a battery of 20 number puzzles designed to test powers of logic and numerical aptitude.

Instructions: In each question a set of numbers within a diagram or set of diagrams is presented. You must study the numbers within the diagrams, decide what pattern or sequence of numbers is occurring and then provide the number or numbers that should replace the question mark(s).

The use of a calculator *is* permitted in this test.

Before commencing the test, work through each of the examples below.

Example 1:

What number should replace the question mark?

Answer: 2

Explanation: In each square add the numbers in the top right, top left and bottom left corners. Then deduct the number in the bottom right corner in order to arrive at the number in the centre. Thus, 3 + 7 + 2 = 12, and 12 – 10 = 2.

Example 2:

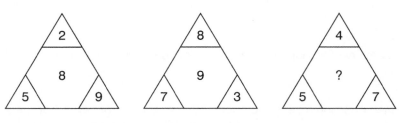

What number should replace the question mark?

Answer: 8

Explanation: In each triangle add the three numbers in the corners and then divide the result by 2 in order to arrive at the number in the centre of the triangle. Thus, $4 + 5 + 7 = 16$, and $16 \div 2 = 8$.

You now have 90 minutes in which to solve the following 20 questions.

Q1

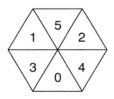 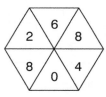 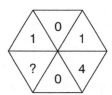

What number should replace the question mark?

Answer [ ]

Q2

What number should replace the question mark?

Answer [ ]

Q3

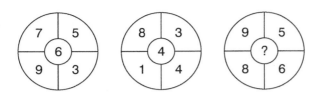

What number should replace the question mark?

Answer

Q4

6	8	3	1
5	2	?	5
3	5	4	6
4	3	5	6

What number should replace the question mark?

Answer

Q5

24	28	42

4	8	2

32	16	32

12	20	?

What number should replace the question mark?

Answer

Q6

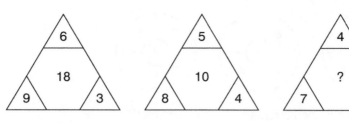

What number should replace the question mark?

Answer

Q7

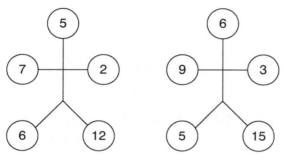

What numbers should replace the question marks?

Answer

Q8

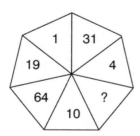

What number should replace the question mark?

Answer

Q9

| 5 | 11 | 23 |

| 7 | 15 | 31 |

| 11 | ? | ? |

| 4 | 9 | 19 |

What numbers should replace the question marks?

Answer

Q10

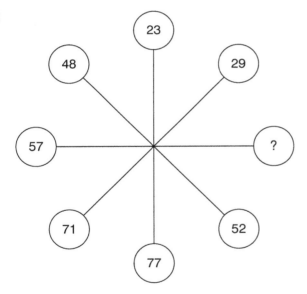

What number should replace the question mark?

Answer

Q11

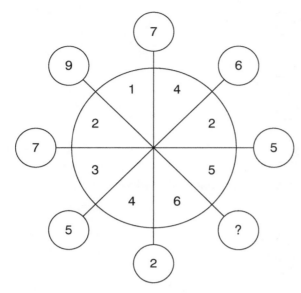

What number should replace the question mark?

Answer

Q12

9	41	57	46	4
25	52	22	13	43
37	29	72	21	48
68	45	17	12	18
36	11	28	39	19

3	10	17	14	26
24	21	37	32	8
13	2	44	20	7
28	15	11	34	18
16	48	23	12	9

Multiply the second-highest odd number in the left-hand grid by the second-lowest even number in the right-hand grid.

Answer

Q13

240	180	135

96	?	?

112	84	63

What numbers should replace the question marks?

Answer

Q14

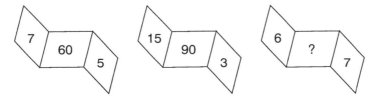

What number should replace the question mark?

Answer

Q15

3	4	7	11	18
2	1	3	4	7
5	5	10	15	25
7	6	13	19	32
12	11	23	34	?

What number should replace the question mark?

Answer

Q16

What number should replace the question mark?

Answer

Q17

	7				3				6	
4	26	3		5	39	3		8	?	4
	2				8				9	

What number should replace the question mark?

Answer

Q18

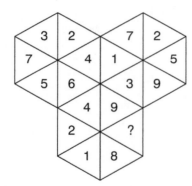

What number should replace the question mark?

Answer

Q19

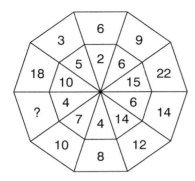

What number should replace the question mark?

Answer _____

Q20

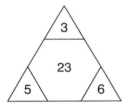 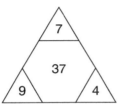 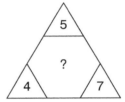

What number should replace the question mark?

Answer _____

Numerical adaptability test

This test is a battery of 10 questions designed to measure your ability to work with numbers and think numerically, and to adapt quickly to different types of questions. It is also a test of your powers of mental arithmetic.

Instructions: The use of calculators is not permitted in this test.

   You should read through each question carefully before it is attempted.

   A time limit of 30 minutes is allowed for completing the 10 questions.

Q1   6, 11, 21, 36, 56, 81, 111, ?

   What number continues the sequence?

   Answer [ ]

Q2   What is 48 multiplied by 15?

   Answer [ ]

Q3   1, 11, 23, ?, 53, 71

   What number should replace the question mark?

   Answer [ ]

Q4

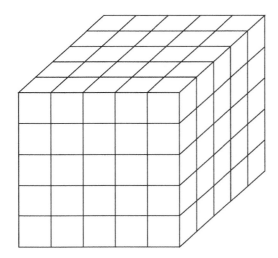

125 square blocks are glued together to form a cube. The cube is then painted red on all six sides. If the 125 blocks are then disassembled, how many blocks will have no paint on them?

Answer [   ]

Q5   What is $\frac{1}{2}$ of $\frac{1}{4}$ of $\frac{1}{3}$ of $\frac{6}{9}$ of 36?

Answer [   ]

Q6   1, 8.5, 23.5, 46, 76, 113.5, ?

What number continues the sequence?

Answer [   ]

Q7   How many minutes before midnight is it, if 90 minutes later it will be as many minutes after 1 am?

Answer [   ]

Q8   7   2   6   9   4   7   3   2   1   7   9   8   4   2   6   5   3   8   2   4

Add up the numbers that appear only once in the above list and multiply the total by the number that appears in the list the most.

What is the answer?

Answer [＿＿＿＿＿＿]

Q9   If a car travels at an average speed of 45 miles per hour when it is moving, how many miles will it travel in 48 minutes if it makes an 8-minute stop at a petrol station during the course of the journey?

Answer [＿＿＿＿＿＿]

Q10   If a lathe rotates at 210 revs per minute (rpm), how many times does it rotate in 1 second?

Answer [＿＿＿＿＿＿]

Geometry test

Geometry is the branch of mathematics that in its most elementary form is concerned with problems such as determining the areas and diameters of two-dimensional figures and the surface areas and volumes of solids.

Because it is not something with which most of us deal on a regular basis it is advisable before taking a numerical aptitude test to brush up on some basic geometric rules, for example:

- The sum of the interior angles of any triangle is equal to the sum of two right angles, a right angle being 90°.

- The square of the hypotenuse (the longest side) of a right-angled triangle is equal to the sum of the squares of the other two sides (Pythagoras' theorem).

The 15 questions in this exercise are designed to test your existing knowledge of basic geometry and at the same time act as a revision to some basic geometric skills, and the methodology and analytical thought processes necessary to solve this type of problem quickly and efficiently.

Instructions: The use of calculators is not permitted in this test.

You should read through each question carefully before it is attempted.

Before commencing the test, work through each of the examples on the following pages.

Example 1:

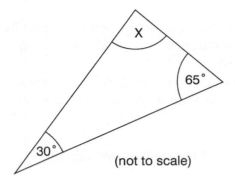

(not to scale)

What is the value of angle x?

Answer: 85°

Explanation: The value (when added together) of the three internal angles in a triangle is always 180°. The two angles for which the value is already given are 30° and 65°. The value of the third angle is, therefore, 180 – (30 + 65) = 180 – 95 = 85°.

Example 2:

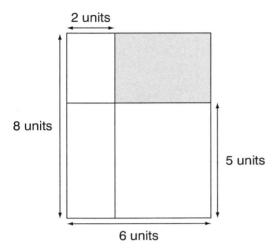

What is the area of the shaded section?

Answer: 12 square units

Explanation:

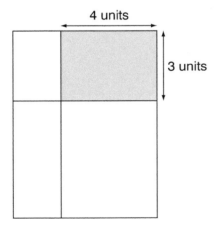

From the information already provided we can work out that the length of the sides of the shaded area is 4 units (6 units − 2 units) and 3 units (8 units − 5 units). The area in square units is, therefore, 4 × 3 = 12 square units.

You have now 60 minutes in which to complete the following 15 questions.

Q1   The area of a cube (whose sides are all equal) is 64 cm³.

What is the length of each side?

A   2 cm   C   6 cm

B   4 cm   D   8 cm

Answer [   ]

Q2

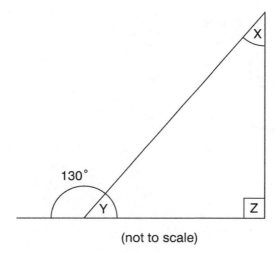

130°

Y

Z

X

(not to scale)

What is the value of angle X?

A   50°   C   40°

B   45°   D   30°

Answer [   ]

Q3

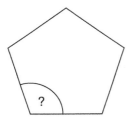

The value of each internal angle of a square is 90°.

What is the value of each internal angle in a pentagon?

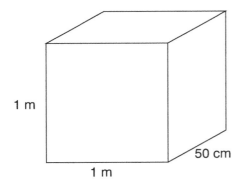

A   96°   C   112°

B   108°   D   120°

Answer

Q4

1 m

1 m

50 cm

The above box measures 1 m × 1 m × 50 cm. How many of these boxes can be fitted into a container whose internal measurements are 10 m × 6 m × 6 m?

Note: 1 m = 100 cm

A   120   C   360

B   144   D   720

Answer

Q5

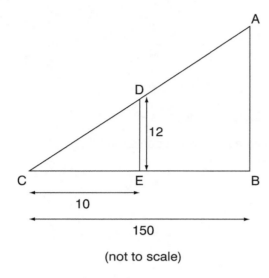

(not to scale)

What is the height of line AB?

A   125 units

B   180 units

C   225 units

D   360 units

Answer _____

Q6

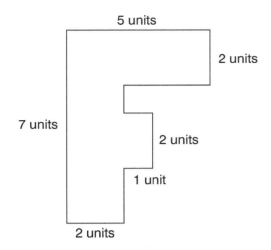

5 units

2 units

7 units

2 units

1 unit

2 units

What is the area in square units of this figure?

A   18 square units

B   19 square units

C   20 square units

D   22 square units

Answer

Q7   If three squares, each 9 cm², are placed end to end to form a rectangle, what would be the length of the rectangle's longest side?

A   3 cm   C   9 cm

B   6 cm   D   12 cm

Answer

Q8

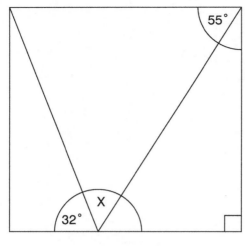

(not to scale)

What is the value of angle X?

A   87°   C   98°

B   93°   D   105°

Answer

Q9

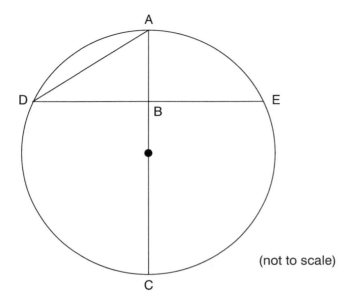

(not to scale)

Line DE crosses line AC at right angles. If line AC travels through the centre of the circle, and the circle has a diameter of 13 cm, what is the length of line AD, given the following additional information:

The length of line BC = 10 cm

The length of line DE = 8 cm

A   4 cm

B   4.5 cm

C   5 cm

D   5.5 cm

Answer _____

Q10

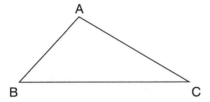

A triangle consists of the intersection of lines AB, AC and BC as illustrated above. Which, if any, of the following dimensioned triangles can be constructed?

A   AB = 6 cm, AC = 1 cm, BC = 5 cm

B   AB = 4 cm, AC = 2 cm, BC = 3 cm

C   AB = 2.5 cm, AC = 4.5 cm, BC = 2.5 cm

D   AB = 10 cm, AC = 20 cm, BC = 25 cm

E   All of the above can be constructed

F   None of the above can be constructed

Answer [   ]

Q11

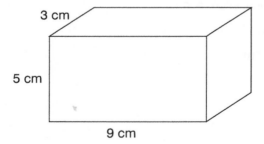

What is the surface area of the above figure?

A   87 sq cm

B   135 sq cm

C   174 sq cm

D   270 sq cm

Answer [   ]

Q12 What is the cubic capacity of the figure in Q11?

A   87 cu cm

B   135 cu cm

C   174 cu cm

D   270 cu cm

Answer

Q13

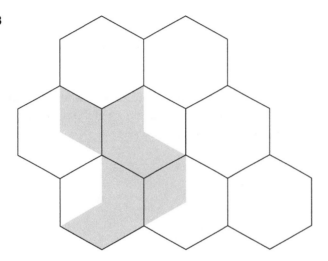

What percentage of the above visible figure is shaded?

A   20%

B   25%

C   40%

D   50%

Answer

Q14

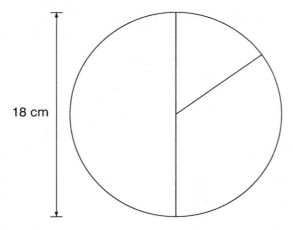

18 cm

The area of a circle is πr^2, and its circumference is $2\pi r$ (where r = radius). Working with π to just two decimal places, that is 3.14, if the above circle has a diameter of 18 cm, what is the area of the circle?

A   25.434   C   254.34

B   56.52   D   565.20

Answer [＿＿＿＿＿＿]

Q15   What is the circumference of the circle in Q14?

A   25.434   C   254.34

B   56.52   D   565.20

Answer [＿＿＿＿＿＿]

Data interpretation test

Data interpretation is becoming increasingly important in industry and commerce, and the exercises that follow test your numerical ability to work with figures and charts and correctly interpret data presented in this format.

Although the use of a calculator is permitted in this test you may at the end of the test find it useful to try interpreting the data without the use of a calculator, by estimating and rounding off sums to convenient amounts and using the data to discover additional information to that extracted in the 10 specific questions below.

Instructions: You have 50 minutes in which to complete the 10 questions. As there are two sets of five questions, with the second set of five questions being more difficult than the first set, it is suggested you pace yourself to spend approximately 20 minutes on the first five questions and 30 minutes on the second five questions.

Questions 1–5

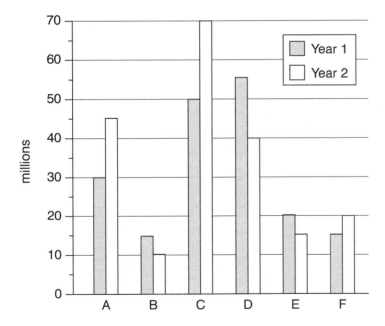

The above graph shows the profit achieved by six companies (A, B, C, D, E and F) over a two-year period.

Q1   Which company increased its profit by the greatest percentage?

Answer [   ]

Q2   Of the companies whose profit dropped, which company had the least percentage drop in profit?

Answer [   ]

Q3   Of the companies whose profit increased, which company had the least percentage increase in profit?

Answer [   ]

Q4   Which company had a 40% increase in profits?

Answer [   ]

Q5   Taking the six companies as a whole, what was the combined total profit or loss in £ millions in Year 2 compared with Year 1?

Answer [   ]

Questions 6–10

The above two graphs show the average monthly rainfall in mm for four towns (A, B, C and D) over a 12-month period.

Q6   Which town had the lowest average monthly rainfall?

Answer [＿＿＿＿＿＿]

Q7   Taking the cumulative total rainfall for all four towns, which was the driest month?

Answer [＿＿＿＿＿＿]

Q8   In which town did the total rainfall from May to August exceed 690 mm?

Answer [＿＿＿＿＿＿]

Q9   Taking the cumulative rainfall for all four towns, which were the three wettest months?

Answer [＿＿＿＿＿＿]

Q10   Which town had the highest average monthly rainfall?

Answer [＿＿＿＿＿＿]

CHAPTER 3

Spatial aptitude

The definition of 'spatial' is 'pertaining to space', and spatial abilities mean the perceptual and cognitive abilities that enable a person to deal with spatial relations. This type of abstract reasoning does not involve problems that are verbal or numerical in nature. The questions within such tests typically take the form of a series of shapes or diagrams from which you have to pick the odd one out, or identify which should come next in a sequence from a set of alternatives, or choose from a set of alternatives which diagram will complete an analogy. The ability being investigated in this type of test is how well a person is able to identify patterns and meaning from what might appear at first glance random or very complex information.

Such tests are referred to as 'culture-free' or 'culture-fair' tests, and are designed to be free of any cultural bias, so that no advantage is derived by individuals of one culture relative to those of another. In other words, they eliminate language factors or other skills that might be closely tied to one particular culture.

When preparing for spatial aptitude tests it will be useful to bear in mind the following points:

- For many people this type of spatial awareness test is a new experience and is not something they are taught at school or college. A considerable amount of practice on the type of questions one is likely to encounter is, therefore, particularly essential.

- At first glance, looking at a page full of seemingly meaningless diagrams may appear daunting. However, by concentrating on each question one at a time calmly the answer may suddenly appear much more obvious than you first imagined.

- Usually even though an option may appear too simple or obvious it is, in fact, the correct answer.

- Unless the question states otherwise, there will be only one correct answer.

- As you practise, try compiling similar types of questions yourself. At first you may even find that it is much easier to compile these types of questions than it is to solve them, but compiling a few questions yourself will increasingly help you to develop the kind of right-hand brain thought processes required to solve them.

Visual odd-one-out test

This test is a battery of 15 questions designed to test appreciation of spatial design and powers of logic, lateral thinking and creativity.

In each set of diagrams you must identify the odd one out, in other words the attribute that the diagram that is the odd one out does not possess or is not shared by the other diagrams.

You should be open minded as to the possible reasons why one of the options is different to the rest. For example, it may be necessary to look for a common theme to every shape or pattern in the question. Perhaps, for example, a small dot appears within a set of diagrams. This presumably is there for a reason and is, therefore, the key to finding the correct solution because in one of the options it appears within a different shape to all the other options.

Another reason may be that four out of the five options are the same figure rotated whilst the remaining option is the odd one out because it is a reflection of the others and not a rotation.

A similar question may contain pairs of identical options that have been rotated or reflected, and the odd one out has not such a pairing. However, it is worth bearing in mind that this can only be a possibility when there is an odd number of options from which to choose.

Instructions: In each of the 15 questions, identify just one option that you think is the odd one out.

Before commencing the test, work through each of the examples on the following pages.

Example 1: Which is the odd one out?

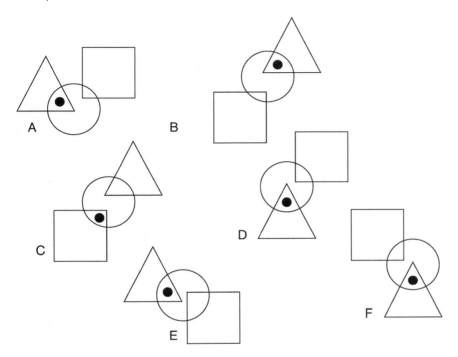

Answer: C

Explanation: In C, the dot is in the circle and square. In the rest it is in the circle and triangle.

Example 2: Which is the odd one out?

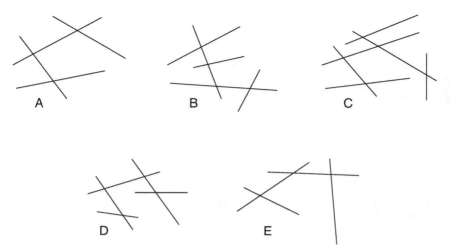

Answer: C

Explanation: Both A and E contain four lines each. Both B and D contain five lines each. As C is the only one to contain six lines, it is the odd one out.

You have now 30 minutes in which to solve the following 15 questions.

Q1   Which is the odd one out?

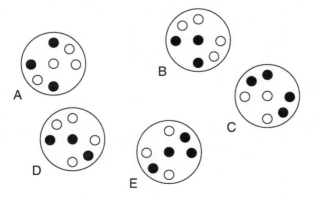

Answer [   ]

Q2 Which is the odd one out?

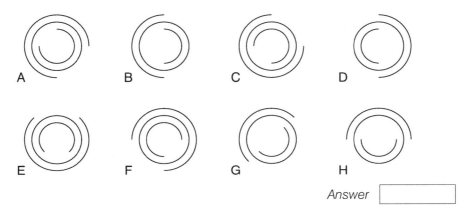

A B C D

E F G H

Answer

Q3 Which is the odd one out?

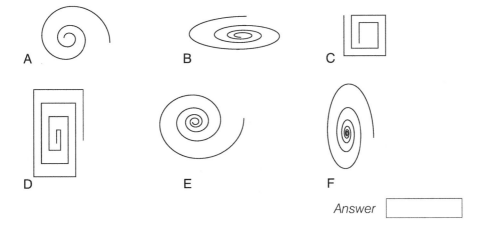

A B C

D E F

Answer

Q4   Which is the odd one out?

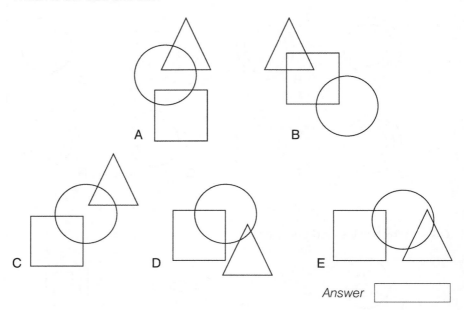

Answer [   ]

Q5   Which is the odd one out?

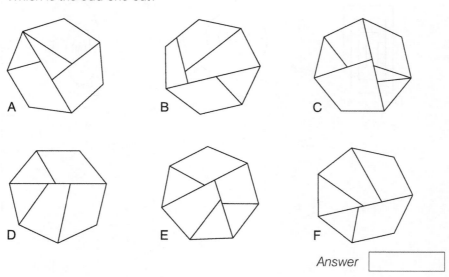

Answer [   ]

Q6   Which is the odd one out?

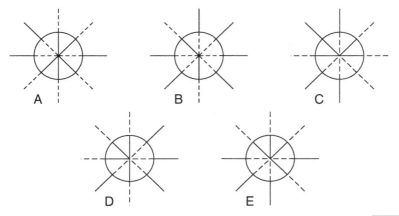

Answer

Q7   Which is the odd one out?

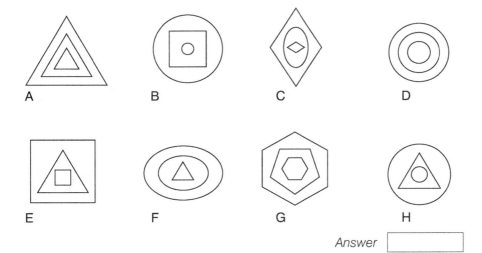

Answer

Q8   Which is the odd one out?

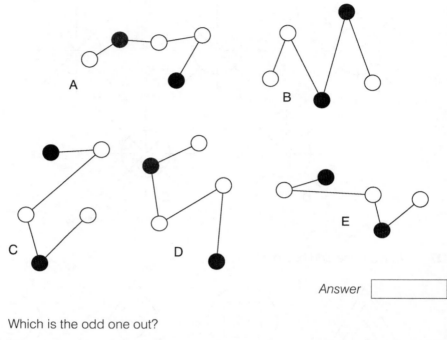

Answer ☐

Q9   Which is the odd one out?

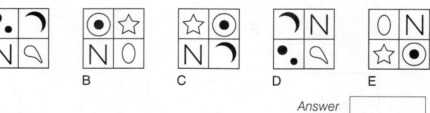

A   B   C   D   E

Answer ☐

Q10   Which is the odd one out?

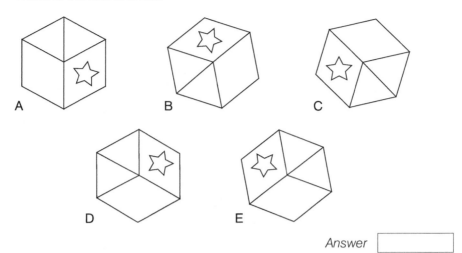

A   B   C

D   E

Answer [   ]

Q11   Which is the odd one out?

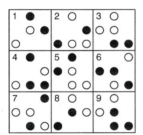

Answer [   ]

Q12   Which is the odd one out?

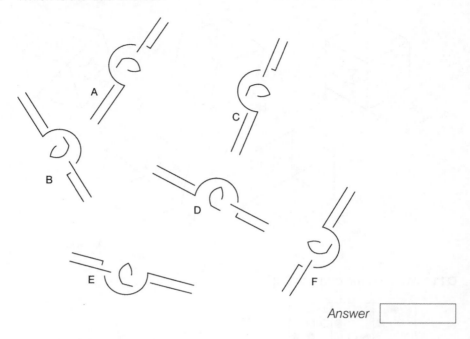

Answer

Q13   Which is the odd one out?

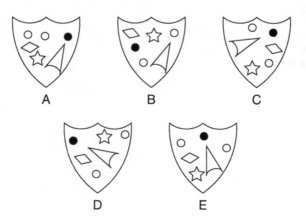

Answer

Q14 Which is the odd one out?

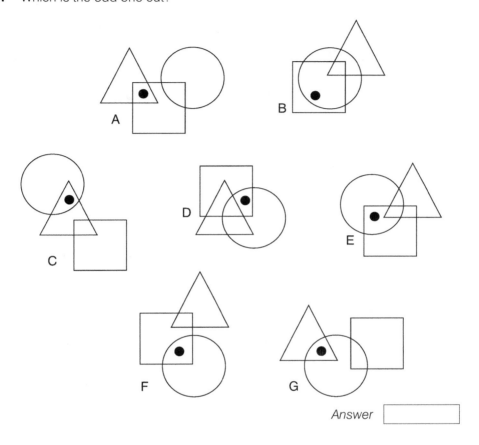

Answer

Q15 Which is the odd one out?

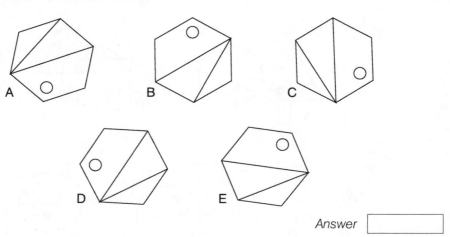

Answer

Progressive matrices test

In a visual matrix test an array of squares is presented with one of the squares (usually the bottom right-hand square) missing, which you have to select from a list of options. It is necessary to study the array as a whole or look across each horizontal line and down each vertical line to work out the logical pattern or progression that is occurring.

As with many spatial intelligence tests many people perform either spectacularly well or spectacularly badly when first encountering this type of test. It is, however, possible to improve your performance considerably by constant practice and by learning to recognize the recurring themes.

One effective method of approaching this type of question, especially as you become more proficient, is to try to work out quickly what you think the missing square (sometimes referred to as the 'missing tile') should look like before studying the options. One disadvantage of looking at the options at the same time as you study the array is that you may become totally confused when seeing the number of different options from which you are asked to choose.

Also, some options may be included purely to add confusion to your train of thought. Take, for instance, option B in example 2 on page 117. This is designed to confuse; for example, why should this be a culmination of all the elements contained in the array? Such confusion could result in the wrong answer being selected, besides which it could cause considerable delay when answering that particular question.

Instructions: Before commencing the test, work through each of the examples below.

Example 1:

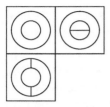

Which tile is missing?

A   B   C   D

Answer: C

Explanation: Looking across, a horizontal line is added to the small circle only. Looking down, a vertical line is added to the large circle only. The tile missing from the bottom right-hand corner should, therefore, contain both a horizontal line inside the small circle and a vertical line inside the large circle.

Example 2:

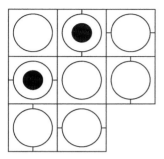

Which tile is missing?

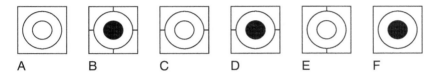

A   B   C   D   E   F

Answer: F

Explanation: Look across each row and down each column. Each row and column of three circles contains one inner black circle, one set of horizontal lines and one set of vertical lines. As the horizontal and vertical lines have already appeared once in the end column and once in the bottom row, the missing tile should contain just the inner black circle within the large circle.

Example 3:

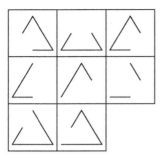

Which tile is missing?

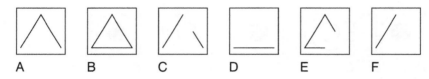

Answer: F

Explanation: The contents of the third square in each row and column are determined by the contents of the first two squares. Lines are carried forward from these first two squares to the third square unless lines appear in the same position in the first two squares, in which case they are cancelled out.

You have now 30 minutes in which to solve the following 15 questions.

Q1

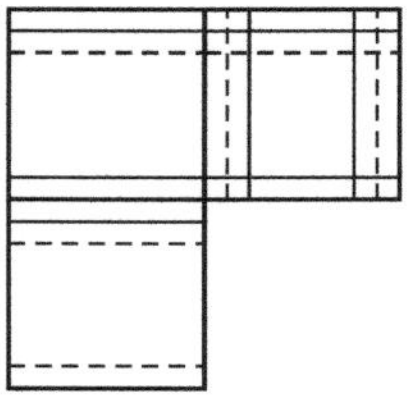

Which tile is missing?

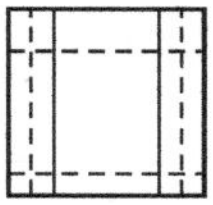

A 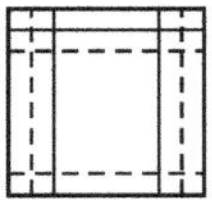   B 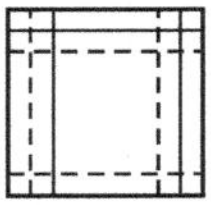   C 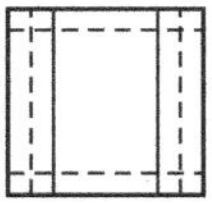   D 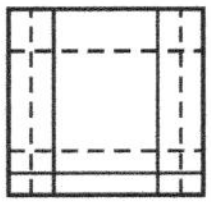   E

Answer

Q2

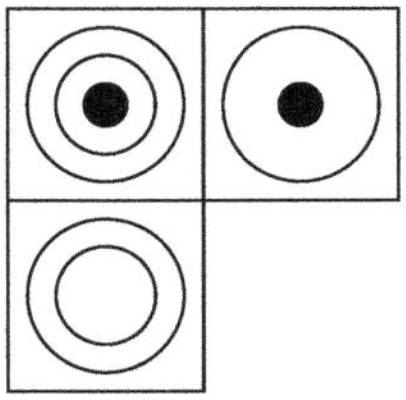

Which tile is missing?

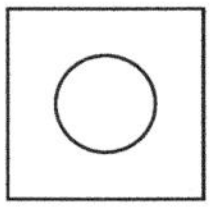

A   B 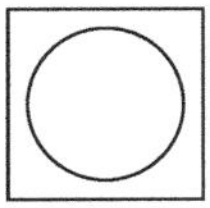   C 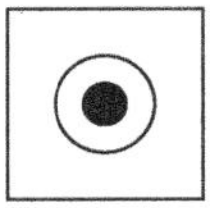   D

Answer

Q3

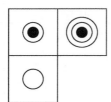

Which tile is missing?

A   B   C   D   E

Answer

Q4

Which tile is missing?

A   B   C   D   E

Answer

Q5

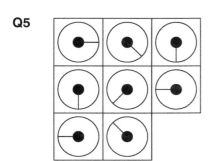

Which tile is missing?

A   B   C   D   E

Answer [   ]

Q6

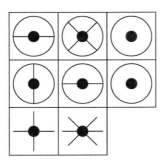

Which tile is missing?

A   B   C   D   E

Answer [   ]

Q7

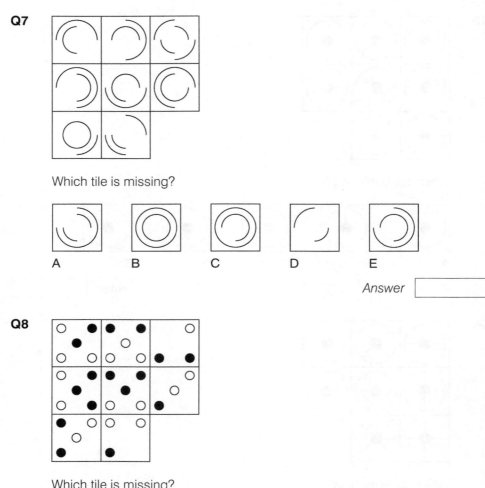

Which tile is missing?

A   B   C   D   E

Answer [   ]

Q8

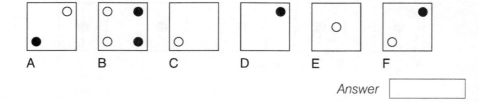

Which tile is missing?

A   B   C   D   E   F

Answer [   ]

Q9

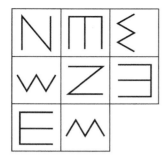

Which tile is missing?

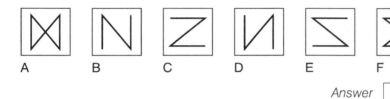

A   B   C   D   E   F

Answer

Q10

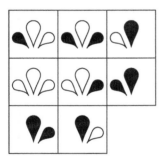

Which tile is missing?

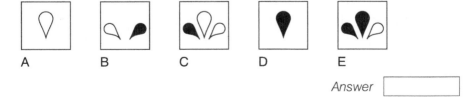

A   B   C   D   E

Answer

Q11

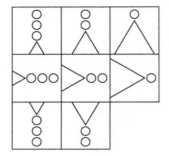

Which tile is missing?

A   B   C   D   E   F

Answer

Q12

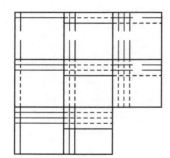

Which tile is missing?

A   B   C   D   E   F

Answer

Q13

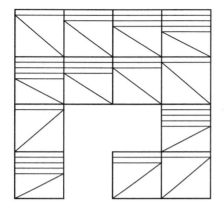

Which tile is missing?

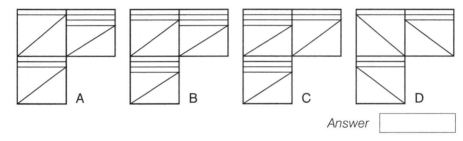

A   B   C   D

Answer

Q14

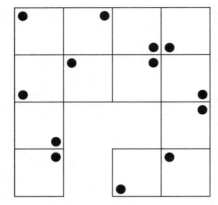

Which tile is missing?

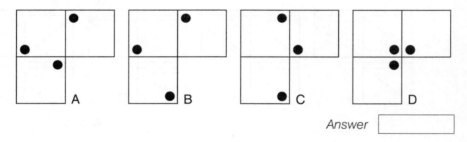

Answer

Q15

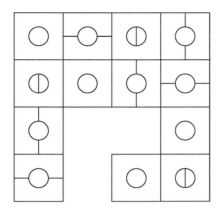

Which tile is missing?

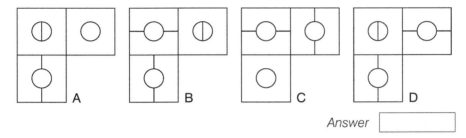

Answer

Visual analogy test

As in the case of a verbal analogy test, in each of the questions in this test it is necessary to reason the answer from a parallel case. In each question you are required to choose, from a set of alternatives, which diagram will complete a similar analogy to the first example.

In certain questions an analogy may be reversed, as in the case of example 1 below where in the first analogy the white dots turn to black and therefore it is correct to assume that in the second analogy, the one you are being asked to complete, the black dots should turn to white.

Instructions: Before commencing the test, work through each of the examples below.

Example 1:

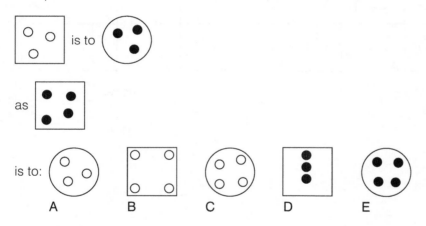

Answer: C

Explanation: The large square containing the dots becomes a circle. The dots turn from white to black or vice versa.

Example 2:

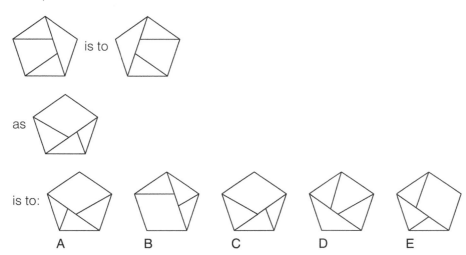

Answer: A

Explanation: The second figure is a mirror image of the first figure.

Note: The mirror image is the same effect as flipping over the figure vertically.

You have now 30 minutes in which to solve the following 15 questions.

Q1

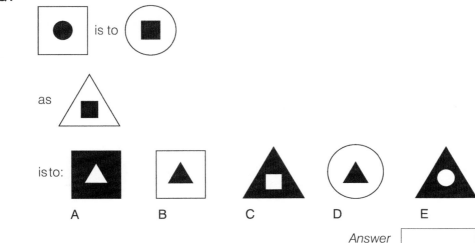

Answer [   ]

Q2

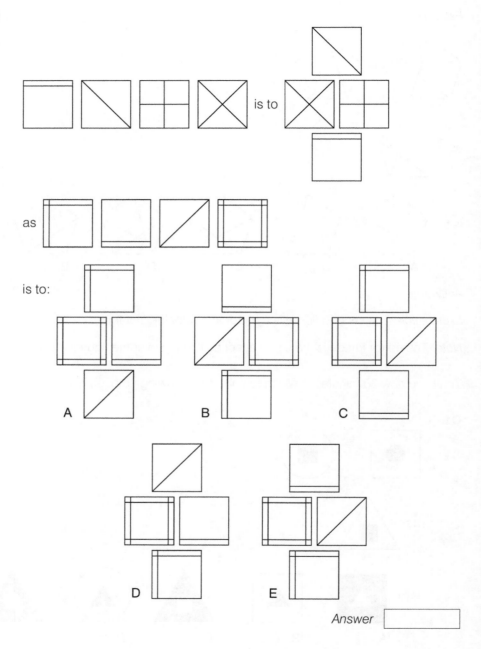

Answer [   ]

Q3

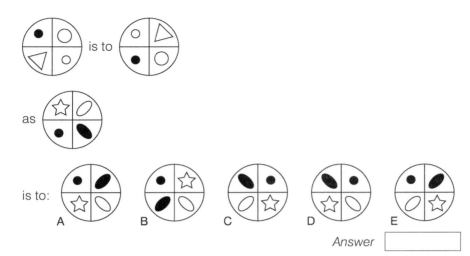

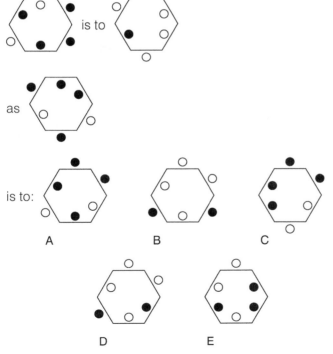

Answer

Q4

Answer

Q5

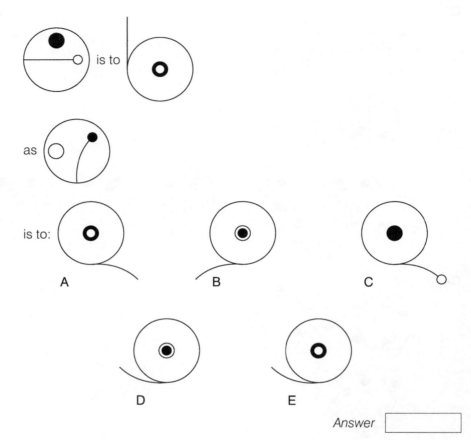

A

B

C

D

E

Answer

Q6

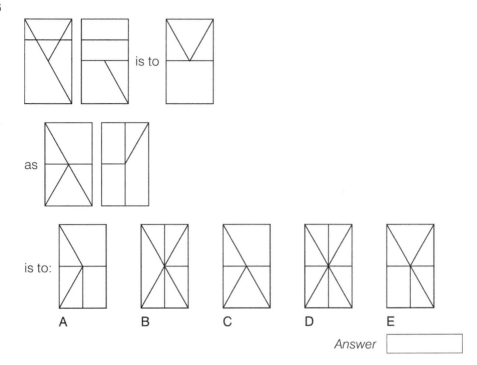

Answer [   ]

Q7

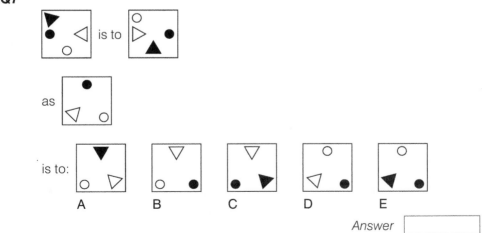

Answer [   ]

Q8

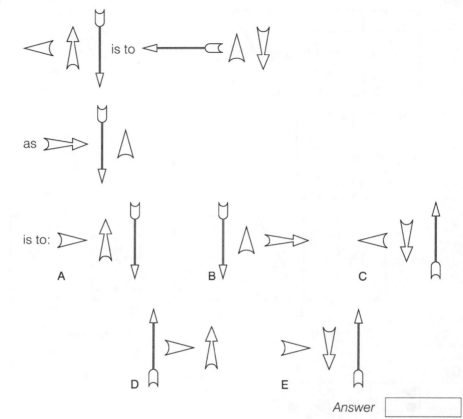

Answer [   ]

Q9

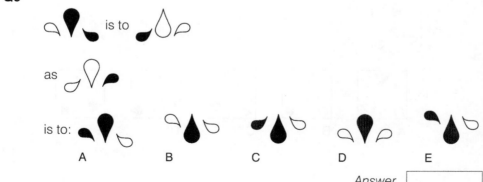

Answer [   ]

Q10

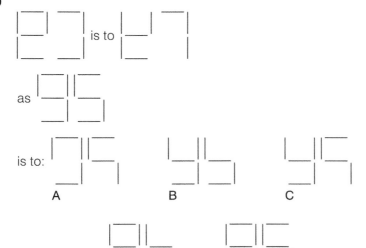

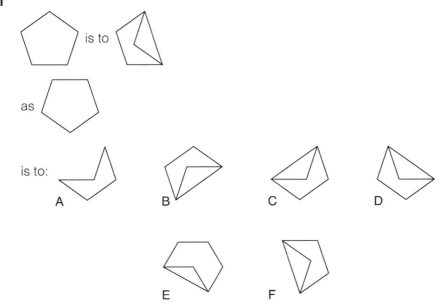

Answer [   ]

Q11

Answer [   ]

Q12

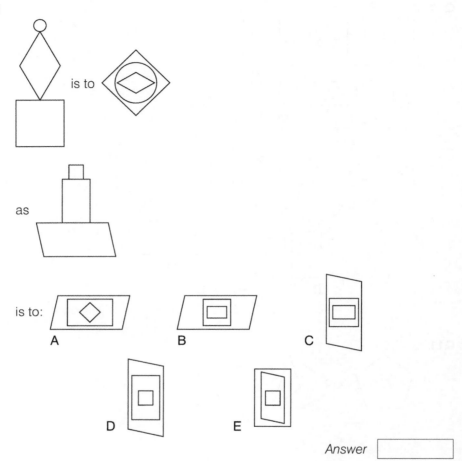

Answer [   ]

Q13

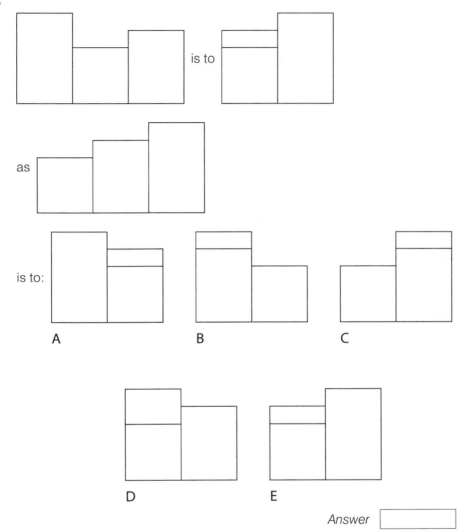

Answer [   ]

Q14

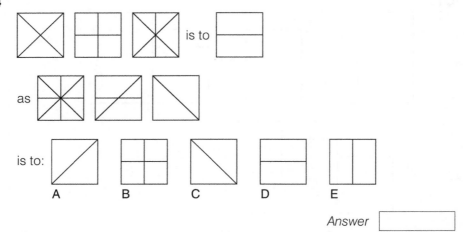

is to:

A   B   C   D   E

Answer

Q15

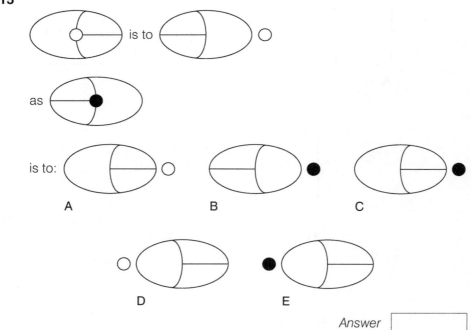

as

is to:

A   B   C

D   E

Answer

Visual sequence test

This test consists of a series of 15 questions in which you are presented with a set of shapes or diagrams that form a logical sequence, and from the information provided you have to choose, from the set of alternatives provided, what comes next in the sequence.

Instructions: Before commencing the test, work through each of the examples below.

Example 1:

Which is the missing figure?

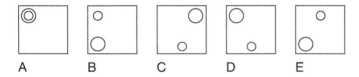

Answer: D

Explanation: The large circle is always situated in one of the corners of the square and is moving one corner anticlockwise at each stage. The small circle is always situated in the middle of one of the sides of the square and is moving one side anti-clockwise at each stage.

Example 2:

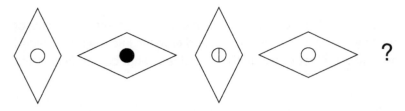

Which is the missing diamond?

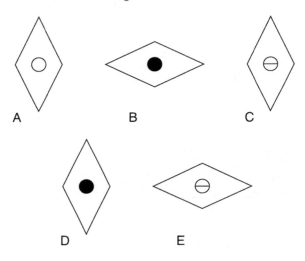

Answer: D

Explanation: The position of the diamond alternates vertical/horizontal. The central dot appears in the sequence white/black/middle line. The next diamond is, therefore, vertical with a black central dot.

You have now 30 minutes to solve the following 15 questions.

Q1

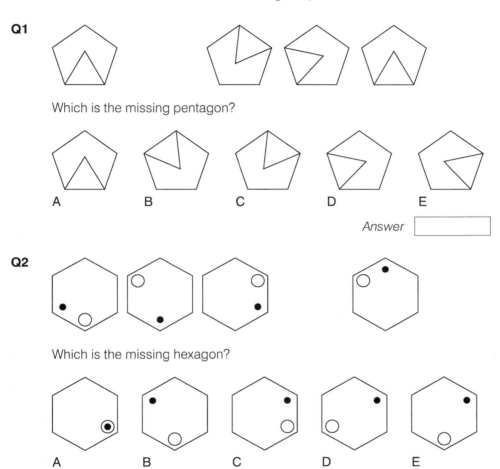

Which is the missing pentagon?

A   B   C   D   E

Answer

Q2

Which is the missing hexagon?

A   B   C   D   E

Answer

Q3

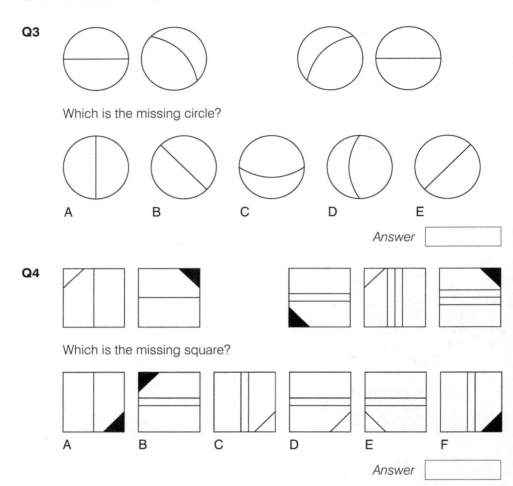

Which is the missing circle?

A   B   C   D   E

Answer [   ]

Q4

Which is the missing square?

A   B   C   D   E   F

Answer [   ]

Q5

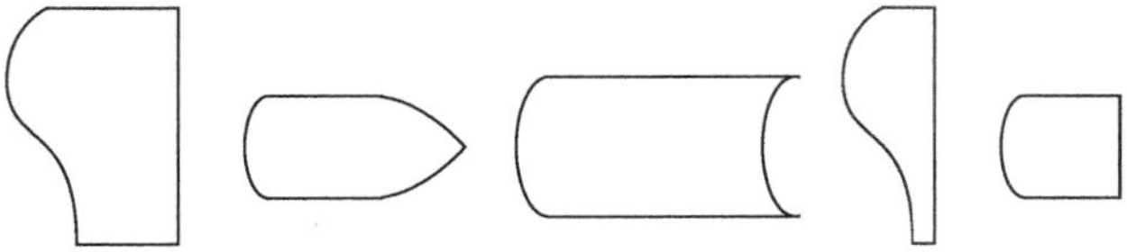

What comes next?

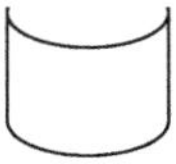

A 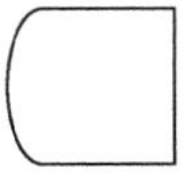   B    C

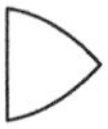

D 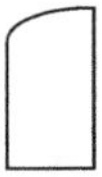   E 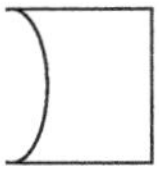   F

Answer [   ]

Q6

What comes next?

A 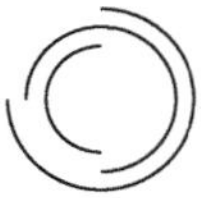   B    C    D 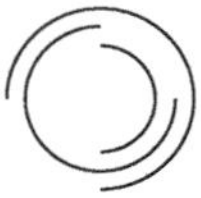   E 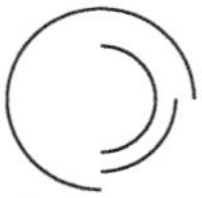   F 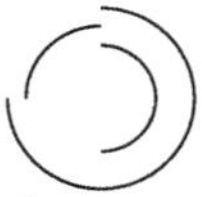   G

Answer [   ]

Q7

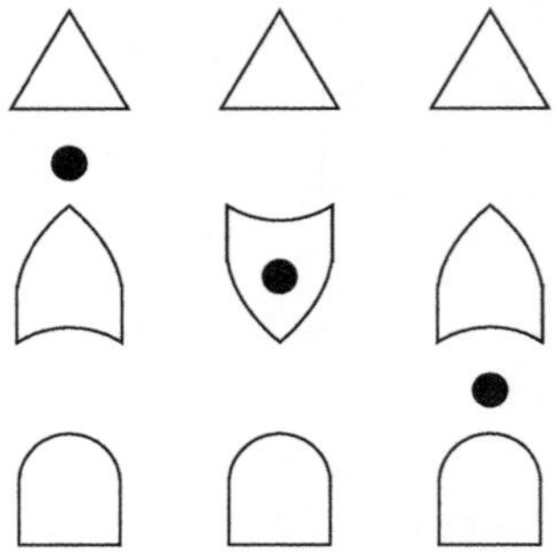

What comes next?

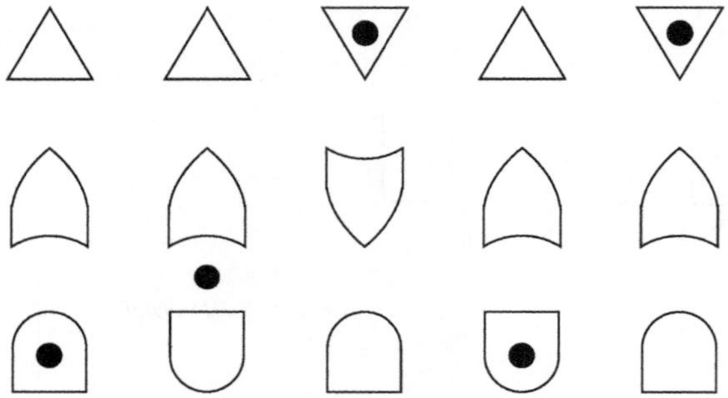

A   B   C   D   E

Answer

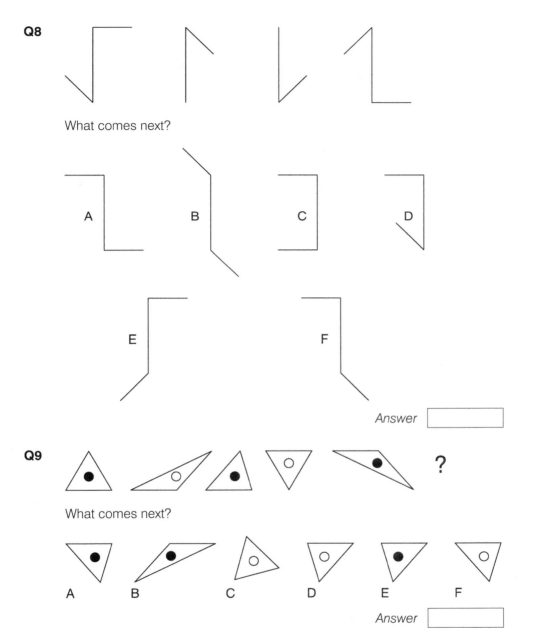

Q8

What comes next?

A
B
C
D

E
F

Answer

Q9

?

What comes next?

A   B   C   D   E   F

Answer

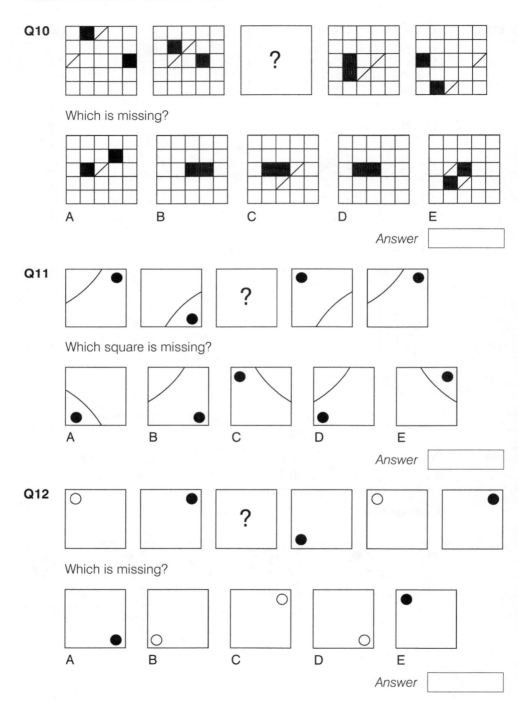

Q10

Which is missing?

A   B   C   D   E

Answer

Q11

Which square is missing?

A   B   C   D   E

Answer

Q12

Which is missing?

A   B   C   D   E

Answer

Q13

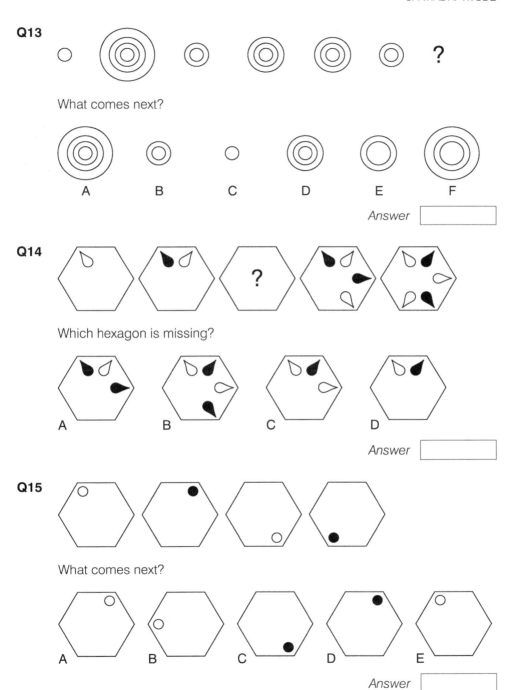

What comes next?

A   B   C   D   E   F

Answer

Q14

Which hexagon is missing?

A   B   C   D

Answer

Q15

What comes next?

A   B   C   D   E

Answer

Shapes test

This test consists of a variety of 10 questions designed to test spatial appreciation, creativity and quickness of mind in adapting to different types of question.

Instructions: As there are several different types of question within the test it is necessary to read the instructions to each question very carefully before attempting it.
Before commencing the test, work through the example below.

Example:

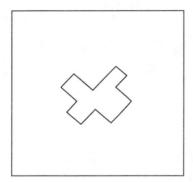

Which piece below will fit in the centre of the square?

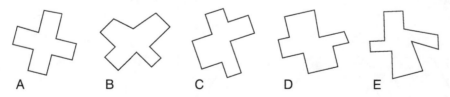

A   B   C   D   E

Answer: C

You have now 20 minutes to solve the following 10 questions.

Q1

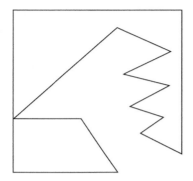

Which shape will complete the square?

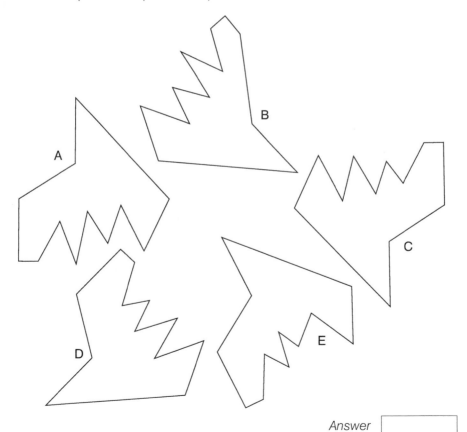

Answer

Q2   Which two figures are identical?

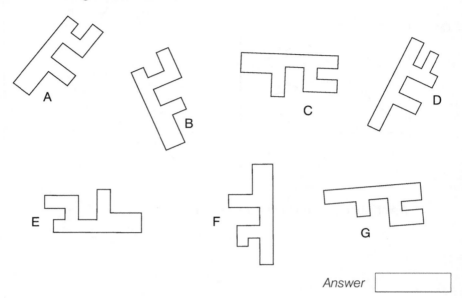

Answer

Q3

Which one of the figures below can be formed by rotating the figure above?

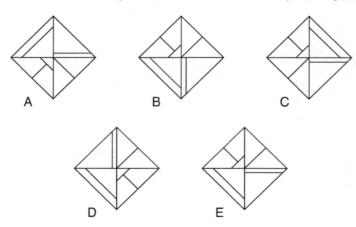

Answer

Q4

Which figure below is a reflection of the figure above and not a rotation?

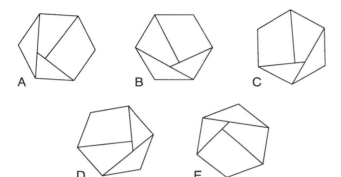

A   B   C

D   E

Answer

Q5

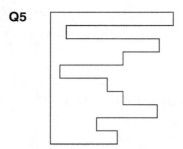

Which figure below when fitted to the figure above will form a perfect square?

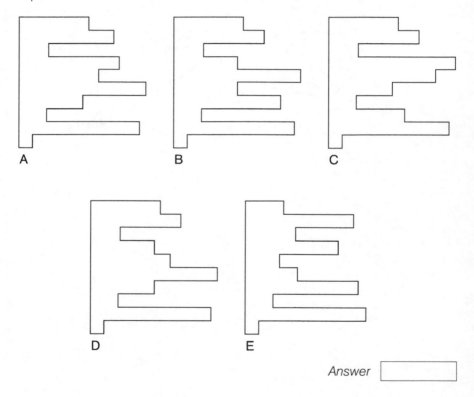

Answer

Q6

Which one of the figures below can be formed by rotating the figure above?

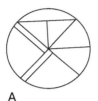

A

B

C

D

E

Answer

Q7

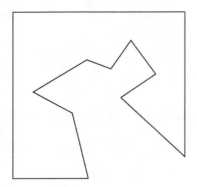

Which shape will complete the square?

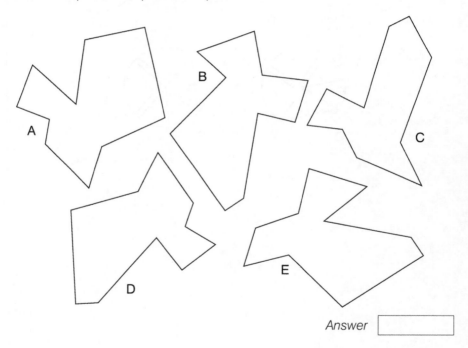

Answer

Q8   Which two figures are identical?

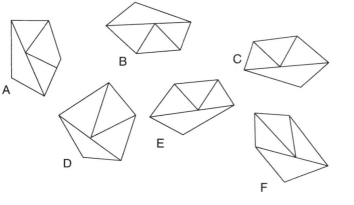

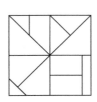

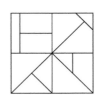

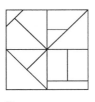

Answer

Q9

Which one of the figures below can be formed by rotating the figure above?

A   B   C

D   E

Answer

Q10

Which figure below is a reflection of the figure above and not a rotation?

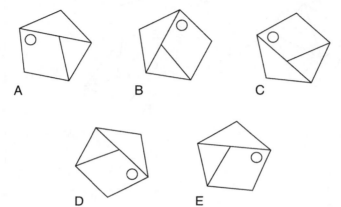

A   B   C

D   E

Answer _____

CHAPTER 4

General IQ tests

Intelligence quotient (IQ) is an age-related measure of intelligence level. The word 'quotient' means the result of dividing one quantity by another, and a definition of intelligence is mental ability or quickness of mind.

Generally such tests consist of a graded series of tasks, each of which has been standardized with a large representative population of individuals. Such a procedure establishes the average IQ as 100.

In contrast to tests of specific proficiencies, intelligence tests are standard examinations devised to measure human intelligence as distinct from attainments. There are several different types of intelligence test, for example Cattell, Stanford-Binet and Wechsler, each having its own different scale of intelligence. The Stanford-Binet is heavily weighted with questions involving verbal abilities and is widely used in the United States of America, and the Wechsler scales consist of two separate verbal and performance sub-scales each with its own IQ rating.

It is generally agreed by advocates of IQ testing that an individual's IQ rating is mainly hereditary and remains constant in development to about the age of 13, after which it is shown to slow down, and beyond the age of 18 little or no improvement is found. It is further agreed that the most marked increase in a person's IQ takes place in early childhood.

IQ tests are standardized after being given to many thousands of people and an average IQ (100) established, a score above or below this norm being used to establish the subject's actual IQ rating. Ideally a properly validated test would have to be given to several thousand people and the results correlated before it would reveal an accurate measurement of a person's IQ.

There are many different types of intelligence tests. However, a typical IQ test would most commonly consist of three sections each testing a different ability, usually comprising verbal reasoning, numerical ability and diagrammatic, or spatial, reasoning.

The questions in the two tests that follow are multidiscipline, each being divided into three sections of 10 questions per section: verbal, numerical and diagrammatic. By structuring the tests in this way the results will determine individual strengths and weaknesses in the three different disciplines being assessed.

Although it is generally accepted that a person's IQ remains constant throughout life and, therefore, it is not possible to increase your actual IQ, it is possible to improve your performance on IQ tests by practising the many different types of question and learning to recognize the recurring themes.

Instructions: Each test contains 30 questions.

You should read the instructions to each question before attempting to solve it.

Before commencing the two main tests, work through the practice test below together with the answers and explanations given.

Practice test: You have 10 minutes in which to solve the following six questions.

Q1   Multiply is to Product as Divide is to: Tangent, Result, Number, Quotient, Share

Answer [   ]

Q2   Which two words are closest in meaning?

triumph, joy, success, wealth, anguish, loyalty

Answer [   ]

Q3   3   (36)   6

4   (40)   5

7   (?)   3

What number should replace the question mark?

Answer [   ]

Q4   100, 99, 97, 94, 90, 85, ?

What number should replace the question mark?

Answer

Q5

What comes next?

A   B   C   D   E

Answer

Q6

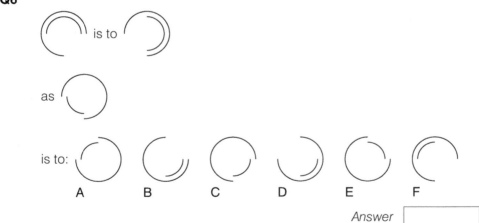

A   B   C   D   E   F

Answer

Answers and explanations:

Q1   quotient

The quotient is the result of dividing; the product is the result of multiplying.

Q2   triumph, success

triumph: a successful ending of a struggle or contest

joy: the emotion of great happiness

success: an event that accomplishes its intended purpose

wealth: the state of being rich and affluent

anguish: extreme mental distress

loyalty: feelings of allegiance

TRIUMPH and SUCCESS are the two words that are closest in meaning.

Q3   42: In each set, multiply the numbers either side of the brackets together and then multiply the result by 2 to obtain the number inside the brackets. Thus, $7 \times 3 = 21$ and $21 \times 2 = 42$.

Q4   79: The amount deducted increases by 1 each time, that is 1, 2, 3, 4, 5, 6.

Q5   E: At each stage a line is added to a side of the triangle internally working clockwise.

Q6   A: The arcs each move 90i clockwise.

For each of the following two main tests you have now 60 minutes per test to solve the 30 questions.

It is suggested that you pace yourself so that you spend approximately 20 minutes on each 10-question section.

It is further suggested that before attempting Test two you mark and analyse your results for Test one.

Test one

Verbal section

Q1 Which word in brackets is closest in meaning to the word in capitals?

DISCOURSE (shame, conflict, channel, dialogue, control)

Answer

Q2 Which word in brackets is most opposite in meaning to the word in capitals?

AUSTERE (unrelenting, unpropitious, sumptuous, wealthy, perceptible)

Answer

Q3 Which two words are closest in meaning?

lacking, deference, respect, specific, protection, rout

Answer

Q4 Identify two words (one from each set of brackets) that form a connection (analogy) when paired with the words in capitals.

QUADRUPED (number, animal, four)

QUATRAIN (verse, year, division)

Answer

Q5 Which two words are most opposite in meaning?

large, potent, feasible, aged, ignoble, weak

Answer

Q6 Which two words are most opposite in meaning?

incisive, critical, illicit, appreciative, proud, bewildered

Answer

Q7 pew is to congregation as pulpit is to: choir, transept, sanctuary, preacher

Answer

Q8 Which is the odd one out?

inaugurate, innovate, culminate, germinate, embark

Answer

Q9 The .... were all presented with ....

....

From the choice below, insert the correct four words into the sentence above.

> personnel   personal   stationery   stationary   there   their

Q10 As she became older and wiser she was able to .... many of her high .... to her pupils, who were ....

.... to her for the rest of their ....

From the choice below, insert the correct six words into the sentence above.

> morel   moral   teach   learn   principals   principles   life   lives
> grateful   greatful   quite   quiet

Numerical section

The use of a calculator is not permitted in this section.

Q11

| 6 | 2 | | ÷ | 7 | = | 1 | 6 | 5 | − | 7 | 6 |

Which is the missing box?

| 2 | 3 | 5 | 7 | 9 |
| A | B | C | D | E |

Answer

Q12 Divide 396 by 9 and add 79.

What is the answer?

Answer [   ]

Q13 What is 7/5 expressed as a decimal?

Answer [   ]

Q14 If A = 2, B = 4, C = 9, D = 5 and E = 7, what letter is missing from the sum below?

$$\frac{C+E}{B} = \frac{(A \times D)+(? \times A)}{(A+B)}$$

Answer [   ]

Q15 Jack is one and a third times as old as Jill. How old are Jack and Jill if their combined ages total 119?

Answer [   ]

Q16 The average of three numbers is 19. The average of two of these numbers is 15. What is the third number?

Answer [   ]

Q17 50, 49, 46, 41, 34, 25, 14, ?, ?

Which two numbers come next?

Answer [   ]

Q18 What is 60% of 240 added to 55% of 120?

Answer [   ]

Q19 Sid and Mary wish to share out £450.00 in the ratio 3:2. How much will each receive?

Answer [   ]

Q20

10	7	14	8	16
26	6	15	60	8
36	24	30	11	12
17	20	42	18	22
10	3	2	5	4

What number is two places away from itself multiplied by 3, three places away from itself plus 2, three places away from itself divided by 2, and three places away from itself less 2? All places referred to are in a straight line either horizontally, vertically or diagonally.

Answer _____

Spatial section

Q21

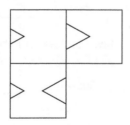

Which is the missing tile?

A　　　　B　　　　C　　　　D　　　　E

Answer _____

Q22

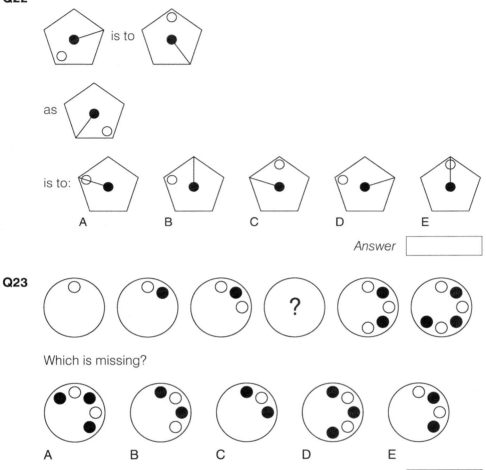

Answer [   ]

Q23

Which is missing?

Answer [   ]

Q24

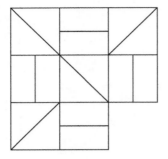

Which is the missing tile?

A B C D E

F G H I

Answer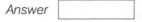

Q25 Which is the odd one out?

A

B

C

D

E

Answer

Q26

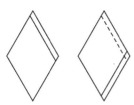 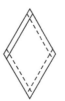 ?

Which is missing?

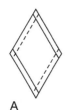 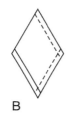  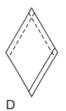 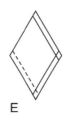 

A   B   C   D   E   F

Answer _____

Q27

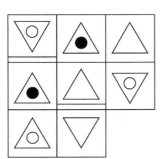

Which is the missing tile?

A   B   C   D   E   F

Answer _____

Q28

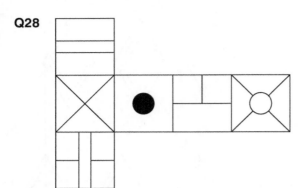

When the above is folded to form a cube, which is the only one of the following that can be produced?

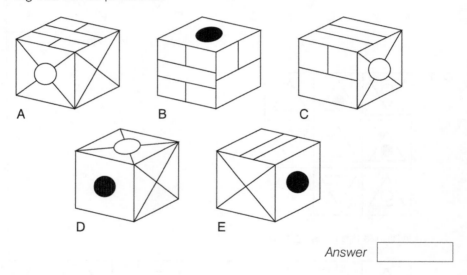

A   B   C

D   E

Answer

Q29

What comes next?

 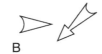

A   B   C

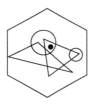

D   E

Answer [   ]

Q30

To which hexagon below can a dot be added so that it then meets the same conditions as in the hexagon above?

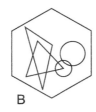

A   B   C

D   E

Answer [   ]

Test two

Verbal section

Q1   Which two words are closest in meaning?

noticeable, salutary, beatific, beneficial, perverse, animated

Answer [   ]

Q2   Which word in brackets is closest in meaning to the word in capitals?

GREEN (vermilion, verdant, cerulean, stygian, aureate)

Answer [   ]

Q3   Which word in brackets is most opposite in meaning to the word in capitals?

PROFICIENT (crude, inept, thoughtless, frugal, reckless)

Answer [   ]

Q4   Which two words are most opposite in meaning?

animated, lethal, innocuous, friendly, prolix, valid

Answer [   ]

Q5   Which is the odd one out?

encounter, forum, quorum, summit, conclave

Answer [   ]

Q6   amplify is to augment as escalate is to: inflate, accrue, spiral, wax, propagate

Answer [   ]

Q7   Which two words are closest in meaning?

advisable, legalistic, theoretical, genuine, strict, phlegmatic

Answer [   ]

Q8   Which word in brackets is closest in meaning to the word in capitals?

GAINSAY (dispute, harvest, wander, achieve, hasten)

Answer [   ]

Q9 Which is the odd one out?

altimeter, thermostat, sextant, theodolite, thermometer

Answer

Q10 Which sentence below is most grammatically correct?

A 'Whose left this on my desk!' exclaimed the headmaster. 'Whose chewing gum is it? Come on now, answer me at once, to whom does it belong?'

B 'Who's left this on my desk?' exclaimed the headmaster. 'Who's chewing gum is it? Come on now, answer me at once, to whom does it belong?'

C 'Who's left this on my desk?' exclaimed the headmaster. 'Whose chewing gum is it? Come on now, answer me at once, to whom does it belong?'

D 'Whose left this on my desk?' exclaimed the headmaster. 'Whose chewing gum is it? Come on now, answer me at once, to whom does it belong?'

E 'Who's left this on my desk?' exclaimed the headmaster. 'Who'se chewing gum is it? Come on now, answer me at once, to whom does it belong?'

Answer

Numerical section

The use of a calculator is not permitted in this section with the exception of questions 14, 15 and 20.

Q11 0, 19, 38, 57, ?, 95, ?

What two numbers are missing?

Answer

Q12 If five men build a house in 28 days, how long will it take eight men to build a house, assuming they all work at the same rate?

Answer

Q13 5, 10, 30, 60, 180, 360, 1080, ?, ?

What two numbers come next?

Answer

Q14   A photograph measuring 10.6 by 8.4 cm is to be enlarged. If the enlargement of the longer side is 26.5 cm, what is the length of the smaller side?

Answer ⬚

Q15   At the end of the day, two market stalls had sold out of everything except cucumbers and cauliflowers. The first market stall had 12 cucumbers and 36 cauliflowers left. The second market stall had 18 cucumbers and 12 cauliflowers left. What is the difference between the percentages of cucumbers left in each market stall?

Answer ⬚

Q16   0, 0, 1, 3, 6, 10, 15, 21, 28, ?

What number comes next?

Answer ⬚

Q17   100, 99.5, 98.5, 97, 95, 92.5, 89.5, ?

What number comes next?

Answer ⬚

Q18

| 9 | | − | 1 | 9 | = | 8 | × | 9 |

Which is the missing box?

| 1 | 3 | 5 | 9 | 7 |
| A | B | C | D | E |

Answer ⬚

Q19   36, 72, ?, 144, 180

What number comes next?

Answer ⬚

Q20

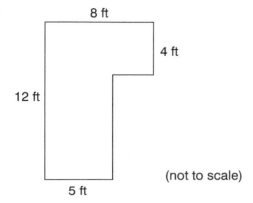

8 ft

4 ft

12 ft

5 ft

(not to scale)

How much does it cost to carpet the above room if carpet costs £10.65 per square foot?

Answer

Spatial section

Q21

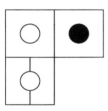

Which is the missing tile?

A   B   C   D   E

Answer

Q22

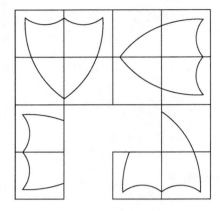

Which is the missing section?

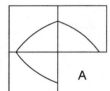

A

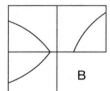

B

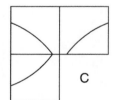

C

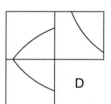

D

Answer

Q23

  ?

Which is missing?

A   B   C   D   E

Answer [   ]

Q24   Which is the odd one out?

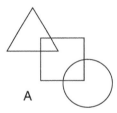

A

B

C

D

E

Answer [   ]

Q25

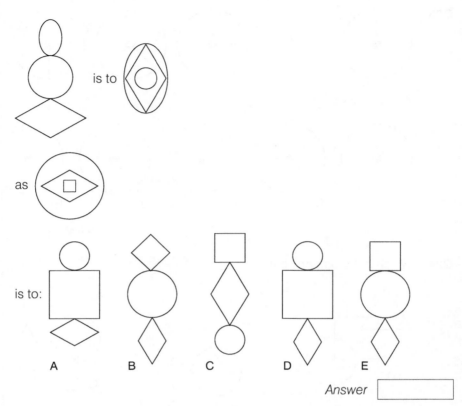

Answer ▢

Q26

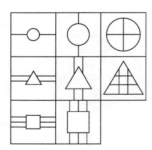

Which is the missing tile?

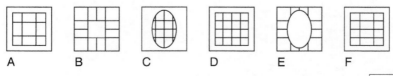

A   B   C   D   E   F

Answer ▢

Q27

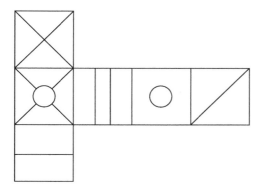

When the above is folded to form a cube, which is the only one of the following that can be produced?

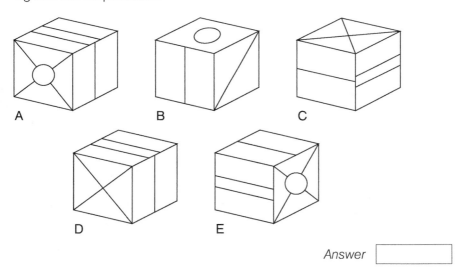

A   B   C

D   E

Answer

Q28

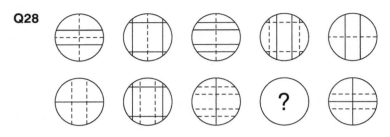

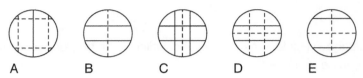

Which circle should replace the one with the question mark?

A   B   C   D   E

Answer

Q29

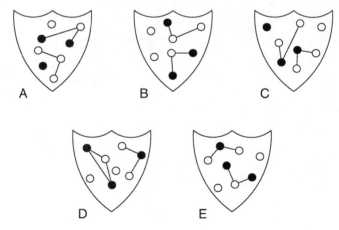

Which shield below has most in common with the shield above?

A   B   C

D   E

Answer

Q30

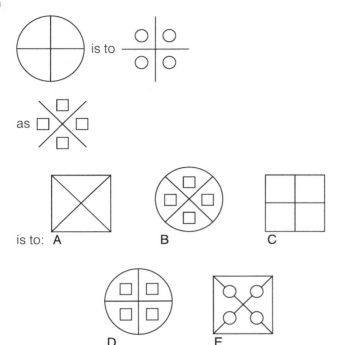

is to: A   B   C

D   E

Answer

CHAPTER 5

Personality testing

Although aptitude testing is an important part of psychometric testing, it is becoming increasingly acknowledged that personality profiling is of equal importance.

Whilst a high score in an aptitude test is desirable and may impress a prospective employer, it does not automatically follow that applicants will be suited to the position for which they are applying. Even though they may be well qualified to do the actual job in terms of both qualifications and intellectual ability, they may underperform if they do not actually enjoy many aspects of the work involved or are unlikely to work well within a team environment or are not sufficiently motivated.

It is likely, therefore, that when attending an interview you will be asked to participate in a personality profiling test. Such a test will measure personality traits, for example how you relate to other people; how you relate to emotions, both your own and your colleagues'; or how well you respond to pressure.

Although personality questionnaires are usually described as tests, they do not have pass or fail scores, nor are they usually timed.

In the case of personality tests, there may be a temptation to try to *beat* the test by determining what the *correct* answer should be. It is, however, important that whenever you are faced with a personality questionnaire you answer each question honestly.

Any attempt to guess the *correct* answer, in other words the answer you think your prospective employer would most like to hear, may well be noticed when your results are analysed or when the face-to-face interview takes place. Also some tests guard against manipulation by posing the same question more than once, but in a different way.

At all times, therefore, testees should follow the instructions and answer each question honestly and openly. In the unlikely event of candidates *beating* the test, then they have not done themselves any favours, as this could result in them being offered a job that does not suit them, and this could be an unfortunate and unhappy start to their career.

The following are some points to bear in mind when completing a personality test questionnaire:

- These types of questionnaire tend not to have *right* or *wrong* answers, nor do they have fixed time limits.

- Do not spend more than a few seconds thinking about the answer to any one question. Answer each question honestly and instinctively, which will usually be the first answer that comes to mind.

- Answer all of the questions.

- If you are unsure about any one question, select the answer that you believe would best describe how you would react in general or how you would react or behave if you were given the choice.

Personality tests may be found in several different formats, of which the following are just a few examples.

Format A

Answer each question or statement by choosing which one of the three alternative responses given is most applicable to you.

For example:

What style of work do you prefer?

a.   working to clearly stated instructions ☐

b.   being left to my own devices ☐

c.   organizing others ☐

Format B

In each of the following tick just one word from the three alternatives provided that you think is most applicable to yourself. You must make a choice in each case to obtain an accurate assessment.

For example:

a.   tentative   ☐

b.   firm   ☐

c.   rational   ☐

Format C

In each of the following choose from a scale of 1–5 which of these statements you most agree with or is most applicable to yourself. Choose just one of the numbers 1–5 in each of the 25 statements. Choose 5 for most agree/most applicable, down to 1 for least agree/least applicable:

For example:

I find it easy to quickly forgive and forget.

5   4   3   2   1

Format D

Answer each question by ticking either the YES or NO box.

For example:

I feel at ease when attending large social gatherings.   ☐ YES   ☐ NO

Format E

Tick just one box for each question.

For example:

	YES	NOT SURE	NO
I value justice more highly than mercy.	☐	☐	☐

Format F

In each of the following, rank the four statements in each group from 1 to 4 according to which is most applicable to yourself, which is least applicable, and which of the remaining two are next most applicable and next least applicable.

For example:

a.   I often say things on impulse that I later regret.   ☐

b.   I talk fast and gesticulate a lot.   ☐

c.   I am not a fast talker but do gesticulate a lot.   ☐

d.   I talk fairly fast but do not gesticulate very much.   ☐

Whilst it is not as crucial to practise on tests of personality as it is on tests of aptitude, the following sample tests are designed to give you a flavour of the type and style of personality questionnaires that may be encountered.

Test 1 Structured or flexible

In each of the following choose from a scale of 1–5 which of these statements you most agree with or is most applicable to yourself. Choose just one of the numbers 1–5 in each of the 15 statements. Choose 5 for most agree/most applicable, down to 1 for least agree/least applicable:

1   I take life as it comes rather than having my life mapped out.

| 5 | 4 | 3 | 2 | 1 |

2   I explore all avenues before committing to solutions of problems.

| 5 | 4 | 3 | 2 | 1 |

3   I rely on my own experiences rather than tried and tested methods.

| 5 | 4 | 3 | 2 | 1 |

4   It is advantageous to search for new solutions to old problems.

| 5 | 4 | 3 | 2 | 1 |

5   I keep things flexible rather than making firm decisions.

| 5 | 4 | 3 | 2 | 1 |

6   I am uncomfortable following petty rules and regulations.

| 5 | 4 | 3 | 2 | 1 |

7   I experiment rather than follow routine procedures.

| 5 | 4 | 3 | 2 | 1 |

8   I go with my gut feeling rather than follow a structured approach.

| 5 | 4 | 3 | 2 | 1 |

9   Experimentation and variety are preferred to detailed planning.

   5   4   3   2   1

10   In a debate I find it easy to appreciate both sides of the argument.

   5   4   3   2   1

11   I speculate about various options rather than making an immediate decision.

   5   4   3   2   1

12   Making changes is preferable to sticking rigidly to a strict routine.

   5   4   3   2   1

13   Flexibility is more important than strict adherence to established rules.

   5   4   3   2   1

14   I am always seeking out new experiences.

   5   4   3   2   1

15   I am more comfortable when keeping my options open, rather than committing to a firm decision.

   5   4   3   2   1

Test 2 Social intelligence

Answer each question or statement by choosing which one of the three alternative responses given is most applicable to you:

1   How important is it for you to get involved in the social life at your place of work?

   a. Not particularly important, although I do sometimes involve myself in some social functions. ☐

   b. I am not particularly interested in the social side of things at my place of work. ☐

   c. I am very keen to get involved in the social life at my place of work. ☐

2   Do you enjoy getting to know people?

   a. Sometimes, although I do not go out of my way to get to know people. ☐

   b. Not really. I sometimes feel uncomfortable talking to people who I have not met before. ☐

   c. Yes, the more people I get to know, the better I feel generally. ☐

3   Which of the following do you generally prefer?

   a. Talking with a group of up to five people. ☐

   b. Talking to someone on a one-to-one basis. ☐

   c. Talking with a group of more than five people. ☐

4   How easy is it for you to make conversation at dinner parties?

   a. It is not always easy. However, I usually contribute to the conversation to some extent. ☐

   b. I find it very difficult to join in the conversation at dinner parties and tend just to listen in to what other people are saying and concentrate on my meal. ☐

   c. Very easy. Part of the enjoyment of a dinner party is the conversation. ☐

5   Which of the following is most effective in getting the best out of people?

a. Support. ☐

b. Drive and motivate. ☐

c. Relate to and understand. ☐

6   How do you prefer to spend your leisure time?

a. Relaxing with family. ☐

b. Relaxing alone. ☐

c. With a group of friends. ☐

7   Are you a good listener?

a. It depends who and what I am listening to. ☐

b. No. ☐

c. Yes. ☐

8   When attending meetings do you tend to:

a. Sometimes join in the discussion or debate, but generally let others do most of the talking. ☐

b. Grab a seat at the back and keep a low profile. ☐

c. Usually join in the discussion with relish. ☐

9   Do you feel at ease in a crowd?

a. Usually but not always. ☐

b. No. ☐

c. Yes. ☐

10   How easy is it for you to make friends?

a. Not particularly easy. However, I do have a few good friends. ☐

b. Very difficult. I have few, if any, very close friends. ☐

c. Very easy. I have a wide circle of friends. ☐

11   How often do you seek advice from others?

    a.   Occasionally, when I think it is advantageous or necessary to do so. ☐

    b.   Rarely or never. ☐

    c.   More than occasionally; it is always a good idea to talk things over with friends and acquaintances whose opinions I value. ☐

12   How often have you sat on committees?

    a.   Occasionally. ☐

    b.   Rarely or never. ☐

    c.   More than occasionally. ☐

13   How easy is it for you to lend someone a sympathetic ear?

    a.   Fairly easy. ☐

    b.   Not easy. It can sometimes be embarrassing listening to other people pouring their heart out. ☐

    c.   Very easy. I like to think that I am able to encourage people to share their problems with me. ☐

14   With which of the following statements do you most agree?

    a.   Success cannot be achieved without a certain degree of unpopularity. ☐

    b.   If you want a job done, do it yourself. ☐

    c.   You do not become a success without the involvement of others. ☐

15   If someone telephoned you asking you to sell Christmas raffle tickets for a worthy cause, which of the following is most likely to be your reaction?

    a.   Maybe agree. ☐

    b.   Decline. ☐

    c.   Very likely agree. ☐

16 With which of the following statements do you most agree?

   a. It is important to know the right people. ☐

   b. It is not possible for everyone to overcome social barriers. ☐

   c. It is possible for everyone to overcome social barriers. ☐

17 If you saw an ex-work colleague in the supermarket who hadn't spotted you would you be most likely to:

   a. Catch their attention and have a brief conversation just to enquire how they are. ☐

   b. Probably not bother catching their attention, and wait to see if they noticed you before speaking. ☐

   c. Be interested in talking to them in order to enquire how they are and also catch up on various events and mutual acquaintances. ☐

18 Do you have any problem expressing your thoughts or feelings to others?

   a. Sometimes. ☐

   b. Yes. ☐

   c. No. ☐

19 Which of the following do you believe is most important for a team to be successful?

   a. Attitude. ☐

   b. Strong positive leadership. ☐

   c. Camaraderie. ☐

20 Do you enjoy being at the centre of events when something needs to be organized?

   a. Sometimes. ☐

   b. Not at all. ☐

   c. Yes. ☐

21   Do you look forward to big social events such as weddings?

   a. Sometimes, but not always.   ☐

   b. No.   ☐

   c. Yes.   ☐

22   How would you prefer to spend Saturday evening?

   a. Go out for a quiet meal with two or three other people.   ☐

   b. Quietly at home with my family.   ☐

   c. At some sort of social gathering such as a party or disco.   ☐

23   How do you think people perceive you: as a loner or a mixer?

   a. Not sure.   ☐

   b. Loner.   ☐

   c. Mixer.   ☐

24   How often are you intolerant of other people's views?

   a. Occasionally.   ☐

   b. More than occasionally.   ☐

   c. Rarely.   ☐

25   How much of your leisure time do you spend socializing with a group of people?

   a. Probably about the same as the average person.   ☐

   b. Very little or none.   ☐

   c. Quite a lot.   ☐

Test 3 Team effectiveness and leadership

Answer each question or statement by choosing which one of the three alternative responses given is most applicable to you:

1   How necessary is strong leadership in the 21st century?

a. There will always be a need for strong leadership.   ☐

b. Cooperation is more important than strong leadership.   ☐

c. Strong leadership is sometimes necessary.   ☐

2   Which of the following words do you think is most applicable to yourself?

a. Cautious.   ☐

b. Flexible.   ☐

c. Respectable.   ☐

3   Which of the following do you prefer?

a. Taking the lead from others.   ☐

b. Organizing.   ☐

c. Being left to my own devices.   ☐

4   Which of the following do you believe is the most important leadership attribute?

a. Experience.   ☐

b. Charisma.   ☐

c. Authority.   ☐

5   What are your views about socializing with your work colleagues after office hours?

a. It does not interest me.   ☐

b. It is something I enjoy doing.   ☐

c. Occasionally it is OK; however, I prefer to switch off from
     work outside of office hours.   ☐

6   With which of the following do you most agree?

    a. Team members should be aware of the consequences of making errors. ☐

    b. Teams and team members are stimulated by being given responsibility. ☐

    c. Team members should continually analyse their performance. ☐

7   What is your reaction to the old adage, 'If it isn't bust, don't mend it'?

    a. Agree. ☐

    b. Don't agree as there is always room for improvement. ☐

    c. Usually agree. ☐

8   How sensitive are you to strong criticism?

    a. Quite sensitive. ☐

    b. I don't mind it as long as it is constructive. ☐

    c. I try not to let it worry me. ☐

9   Does the thought of having power over others stimulate you?

    a. Yes. ☐

    b. Never. ☐

    c. Sometimes. ☐

10   With which of the following statements do you most agree?

    a. It is more important for team members to have their own defined areas of responsibility than to have someone in overall control. ☐

    b. In each team there should be someone in charge or overall control. ☐

    c. The best team leaders have the charisma necessary to stimulate their team. ☐

11   Which is the greatest evil?

    a. A technically under-qualified team leader. ☐

    b. An over-intrusive team leader. ☐

    c. A team leader who is overcautious and hesitant about making firm decisions. ☐

12 With which of the following statements do you most agree?

    a. A team is at its strongest when working well within itself. ☐

    b. A team is at its strongest when its purpose is in line with all its members' wants and needs. ☐

    c. A team is at its strongest when the objectives set may at first glance appear too difficult to achieve. ☐

13 Which of the following do you believe is the most important leadership quality?

    a. To be liked and respected by team members. ☐

    b. To offer encouragement and support to team members. ☐

    c. To be able to minimize conflict between team members. ☐

14 Have you ever served on a committee?

    a. No. ☐

    b. Yes, as chair. ☐

    c. Yes, as a committee member. ☐

15 Do you believe people ever follow your example?

    a. Not particularly. ☐

    b. Yes. ☐

    c. Perhaps occasionally. ☐

16 Do you believe that to get the best out of people you should drive them or support them?

    a. Drive. ☐

    b. Both. ☐

    c. Support. ☐

17 Would you prefer to be in control, or go with the flow?

    a. Go with the flow. ☐

    b. In control. ☐

    c. No preference. ☐

18   With which of the following do you most agree?

a.   Regular team meetings are essential in order to evaluate performance continually and reappraise goals.   ☐

b.   Team goals should be clearly stated from the outset.   ☐

c.   Teams should never be afraid of change.   ☐

19   Which of the following do you consider the most important factor towards possessing good leadership skills?

a.   Leading by example.   ☐

b.   People skills.   ☐

c.   The ability to communicate.   ☐

20   With which of the following statements do you most agree?

a.   Team members should be equally adept at doing any job within a team.   ☐

b.   Leaders should channel all their energies into fulfilling all the needs and objectives of their team.   ☐

c.   One of the greatest motivators is responding to a challenge.   ☐

CHAPTER 6

Answers and explanations

Verbal aptitude

Synonym test A *(p 11)*

Answers

Q1	adoption	**Q11**	flavourless
Q2	genuine	**Q12**	futile
Q3	symbolic	**Q13**	slur
Q4	overpower	**Q14**	opening
Q5	wonder	**Q15**	vitriolic
Q6	impartial	**Q16**	quirk
Q7	ruler	**Q17**	tangle
Q8	vain	**Q18**	unleash
Q9	spirit	**Q19**	sequence
Q10	join	**Q20**	defamatory

Performance rating

Score 1 point for each correct answer.

Total Score	Rating	Percentage of Population
19 / 20	genius level	top 5%
17 / 18	high expert	top 10%
15 / 16	expert	top 30%
13 / 14	high average	top 40%
11 / 12	middle average	top 60%
9 / 10	low average	bottom 40%
7 / 8	borderline low	bottom 30%
5 / 6	low	bottom 10%
0 / 4	very low	bottom 5%

Synonym test B (p 14)

Answers

Q1   obtrusive, prying

Q2   profuse, bountiful

Q3   intrepid, audacious

Q4   obtuse, blunt

Q5   range, gamut

Q6   gelid, glacial

Q7   foist, impose

Q8   rift, schism

Q9   rectify, adjust

Q10   brackish, salty

Q11   assiduous, diligent

Q12   cognate, similar

Q13   facet, aspect

Q14   finite, limited

Q15   revere, worship

Q16   tedium, banality

Q17   precept, rule

Q18   static, immobile

Q19   luminary, dignitary

Q20   nosegay, posy

Performance rating

Score 1 point for each correct answer.

Total Score	Rating	Percentage of Population
19 / 20	genius level	top 5%
17 / 18	high expert	top 10%
15 / 16	expert	top 30%
13 / 14	high average	top 40%
11 / 12	middle average	top 60%
9 / 10	low average	bottom 40%
7 / 8	borderline low	bottom 30%
5 / 6	low	bottom 10%
0 / 4	very low	bottom 5%

Antonym test A (p 17)

Answers

Q1	thoughtless		**Q11**	kinetic
Q2	servitude		**Q12**	subjugate
Q3	coherent		**Q13**	inclined
Q4	unimaginable		**Q14**	besmirched
Q5	monotony		**Q15**	multiply
Q6	direct		**Q16**	confirm
Q7	esteem		**Q17**	saunter
Q8	ignorant		**Q18**	rear
Q9	pressing		**Q19**	invariable
Q10	morose		**Q20**	differ

Performance rating

Score 1 point for each correct answer.

Total Score	Rating	Percentage of Population
19 / 20	genius level	top 5%
17 / 18	high expert	top 10%
15 / 16	expert	top 30%
13 / 14	high average	top 40%
11 / 12	middle average	top 60%
9 / 10	low average	bottom 40%
7 / 8	borderline low	bottom 30%
5 / 6	low	bottom 10%
0 / 4	very low	bottom 5%

Antonym test B (p 20)

Answers

Q1 dominant, subsidiary

Q2 verbose, laconic

Q3 coincidental, planned

Q4 stolid, passionate

Q5 flagrant, subtle

Q6 pastel, vivid

Q7 astute, unperceptive

Q8 please, vex

Q9 tasteful, tawdry

Q10 brusque, polite

Q11 systematic, haphazard

Q12 waive, pursue

Q13 fractious, affable

Q14 voracious, temperate

Q15 bliss, heartbreak

Q16 obligatory, optional

Q17 honour, ignominy

Q18 soar, plummet

Q19 diligent, careless

Q20 daunt, encourage

Performance rating

Score 1 point for each correct answer.

Total Score	Rating	Percentage of Population
19 / 20	genius level	top 5%
17 / 18	high expert	top 10%
15 / 16	expert	top 30%
13 / 14	high average	top 40%
11 / 12	middle average	top 60%
9 / 10	low average	bottom 40%
7 / 8	borderline low	bottom 30%
5 / 6	low	bottom 10%
0 / 4	very low	bottom 5%

Analogy test A (p 23)

Answers

Q1	That	**Q11**	Filament
Q2	Impression	**Q12**	Perform
Q3	Weight	**Q13**	Thirty
Q4	Cargo	**Q14**	Gatehouse
Q5	River	**Q15**	Judicious
Q6	Club	**Q16**	Boil
Q7	Places	**Q17**	Gyrate
Q8	Pollute	**Q18**	Floor
Q9	Elaborate	**Q19**	Swing
Q10	November	**Q20**	Cell

Performance rating

Score 1 point for each correct answer.

Total Score	Rating	Percentage of Population
19 / 20	genius level	top 5%
17 / 18	high expert	top 10%
15 / 16	expert	top 30%
13 / 14	high average	top 40%
11 / 12	middle average	top 60%
9 / 10	low average	bottom 40%
7 / 8	borderline low	bottom 30%
5 / 6	low	bottom 10%
0 / 4	very low	bottom 5%

Analogy test B (p 26)

Answers

Q1	Friday, March		**Q11**	work, riches
Q2	channel, isthmus		**Q12**	retrieve, resuscitate
Q3	sphere, cube		**Q13**	jacket, cloak
Q4	thread, ink		**Q14**	power, resistance
Q5	lust, anger		**Q15**	corolla, pedicle
Q6	announce, claim		**Q16**	triangle, quadrilateral
Q7	tree, seam		**Q17**	table, court
Q8	worship, glorify		**Q18**	arm, foot
Q9	window, roof		**Q19**	circles, angles
Q10	cultivated, urbane		**Q20**	green, brown

Performance rating

Score 1 point for each correct answer.

Total Score	Rating	Percentage of Population
19 / 20	genius level	top 5%
17 / 18	high expert	top 10%
15 / 16	expert	top 30%
13 / 14	high average	top 40%
11 / 12	middle average	top 60%
9 / 10	low average	bottom 40%
7 / 8	borderline low	bottom 30%
5 / 6	low	bottom 10%
0 / 4	very low	bottom 5%

Comprehension test 1 – word changes (p 29)

Answers

Q1 **Whenever** asking for **something** face to face it is important to **maintain** eye **contact**.

Q2 In recent **years** there has been a **rapid** increase in fly-on-the-wall **documentary series** and quiz **shows**.

Q3 Many writers keep **notepads** at their **bedsides** and force **themselves** to arouse from their half-sleep and jot these ideas, **dreams** and creative **thoughts** down.

Q4 In order to fully **understand** ourselves we need to **recognize** and **know** ourselves for what we are, rather than what we would like to **be**.

Q5 At last they came to a **spot** a **little** way from the **main road**, and yet so easily seen that no one would miss it.

Q6 Good **judgement** is **generally** much more **desirable** and is **likely** to achieve much **better results** than **acting** on **impulse**.

Q7 The **sea spread** out in all its **beauty** before them, **looking** as **blue** as the sky.

Q8 Past **experiences** enable us to **live** for today and provide the **foundations** on which we can **build** for the future.

Q9 On his **first** visit to the zoo the **young** child reacted with surprise at the number of **different** creatures that lived in the world.

Q10 Technological **change** is now taking **place** at such a **rapid rate** that most of us are at least one **step** behind with the **latest** gadgets and innovations.

Q11   **While** a team does consist of individuals, it **is** only **when** these **individuals** pull together as a team towards a common goal that the **team can** really **be** effective.

Q12   He liked **observing people**, **assessing** their **personalities**, finding out more about them and continually **widening** his **circle** of **friends**.

Q13   The **restaurant** served a **full** range of soups from **consommé** to **heavy-bodied** soups such as oxtail.

Q14   The long leaves of the **dandelion** are **notched**, rather like a **rough** saw, and grow in a **tuft** at the **crown** of a short **stem**.

Q15   He was **ambitious** and saw his **career**, not just as his **way** of life, but as a **gateway** to **creating wealth** and **prominence**.

Performance rating

Score 1 point for each two words correctly placed plus a bonus 3 points for each completely correct sentence.

Total Score	Rating	Percentage of Population
76 / 84	genius level	top 5%
68 / 75	high expert	top 10%
60 / 67	expert	top 30%
52 / 59	high average	top 40%
44 / 51	middle average	top 60%
36 / 43	low average	bottom 40%
28 / 35	borderline low	bottom 30%
20 / 27	low	bottom 10%
0 / 19	very low	bottom 5%

Comprehension test 2 (p 33)

Answers

Q1   For **many** people, **having** more **control**, not just over their **own lives** but **those around** them, means they **feel** less **stress**, although this can have the **reverse effect** if and when it is **brought** home to them how **little**, in **fact**, they **do** control.

Q2   In the **spring countless numbers** of **young** eels **come up** the rivers and then, in **cold weather**, **return** to the **estuaries**, **where** they **bury them-selves** in the **mud**.

Q3   **Change** has **always** been **inevitable**, but **today changes** in lifestyle, attitudes and **technology mean** that this change is **taking place** at an **even greater rate** than **ever before**.

Q4   It **seemed** like a very **good idea** at the **time** but **proved impracticable** when **thought through carefully** and **slept** upon.

Q5   In some puzzles **certain assumptions** must be **made**, for example that **trains arrive** at their **destinations precisely** on **time**. Such puzzles, therefore, can only **work** in **theory**.

Performance rating

Score 1 point for each word correctly placed plus a bonus of 5 points for each completely correct sentence.

Total Score	Rating	Percentage of Population
76 / 88	genius level	top 5%
68 / 75	high expert	top 10%
60 / 67	expert	top 30%
52 / 59	high average	top 40%
44 / 51	middle average	top 60%
36 / 43	low average	bottom 40%
28 / 35	borderline low	bottom 30%
20 / 27	low	bottom 10%
0 / 19	very low	bottom 5%

Classification (p 36)

Answers

Q1   nonsense: it is an absurdity – the rest are all types of expression or turns of phrase

Q2   extemporize: it means improvise – all the other words are related to expanding

Q3   cosmos: it refers to the universe – the rest all relate to time

Q4   serene: it means quiet and calm – the rest mean quiet and thoughtful

Q5   deprave: it means spoil or corrupt morally – the rest mean spoil by making impure or dirty

Q6   violin: it is a string instrument – the rest are wind instruments

Q7   scalpel: it is a surgical instrument – the rest are measuring instruments

Q8 chasm: it is a deep gap – the rest are small gaps or openings

Q9 snag: it is a minor obstacle – the rest are more serious difficulties

Q10 primary: it means the first – the rest all mean the last

Q11 perennial: it means permanent – the rest mean temporary

Q12 thirty seconds: it is half of a minute – the rest are quarter measurements; ninety degrees = ¼ circle, fifteen minutes = ¼ hour, thirteen weeks = ¼ year, twenty-five per cent = ¼ of unity

Q13 sunder: it means break – the rest mean soften

Q14 lobe: it is part of the ear – the rest are part of the eye

Q15 brown – the rest are colours of the rainbow

Q16 table – the rest are all specifically for sitting on

Q17 treble: it is a clef – the rest are all notes

Q18 scold: it means to reprimand – the rest mean to ridicule or poke fun at

Q19 inconceivable: it means impossible – the rest mean difficult

Q20 amend: it means to change – the rest mean to withdraw or delete completely

Performance rating:

Score 1 point for each correct answer.

Total Score	Rating	Percentage of Population
19 / 20	genius level	top 5%
17 / 18	high expert	top 10%
15 / 16	expert	top 30%
13 / 14	high average	top 40%
11 / 12	middle average	top 60%
9 / 10	low average	bottom 40%
7 / 8	borderline low	bottom 30%
5 / 6	low	bottom 10%
0 / 4	very low	bottom 5%

Letter sequences (p 39)

Answers

Q1 LSX: The first and third letters move one forward in the alphabet and the second letter moves one back.

Q2 O: Looking across, miss one letter, that is: EfGhI. Looking down, miss two letters, that is: EfgHijK.

Q3   P   R: Miss one letter and then two letters alternately: AbCdeFgHijKlMnoPqR.

Q4   F   G   H: Miss a letter between each line: AbCDeFGHiJKLMnOPQRS.

Q5   C: Looking across miss one letter, then two and then one: AbCdeFgH. Looking down, miss two letters, then one and then two: AbcDeFghI.

Q6   OL: The first of the two letters works forward through the alphabet in the sequence AbCdeFghiJklmnO. The second of the two letters moves back through the alphabet in the sequence ZyXwvUtsrQponmL.

Q7   EFHG: Each block of four letters starts ABCDE in turn. Each block of four letters contains four consecutive letters of the alphabet but with the third and fourth letters reversed, that is ABCD becomes ABDC.

Q8   S: The sequence progresses AbcdefGhijkLmnoPqrS.

Q9   ST: The sequence progresses ABcDEfgHIjklMNopqrST.

Q10 CX: The first letter of each pair progresses in the sequence: MLkJihGfedC. The second letter progresses in the sequence: NOpQrsTuvwX.

Performance rating

Score 1 point for each correct answer.

Total Score	Rating	Percentage of Population
9 / 10	genius level	top 5%
8	high expert	top 10%
7	expert	top 30%
6	high average	top 40%
5	middle average	top 60%
4	low average	bottom 40%
3	borderline low	bottom 30%
2	low	bottom 10%
0 / 1	very low	bottom 5%

Multidiscipline verbal test (p 42)

Answers

Q1   gap

Q2   The defendant sought **advice** from his **counsel** whether he should plead guilty or not guilty.

Q3   The **eminent** professor warned about the **imminent** dangers of global warming.

Q4   The salespeople who met their targets were rewarded with a bonus.

Q5   austerity

Q6   The **lightning** strike, which had the **effect** of **lightening** up the whole sky, was followed by an angry rumble of thunder.

Q7   It was important that the correct **number** of items were chosen from the **amount** of goods on offer.

Q8   The **emigrant** workers who left Great Britain for new jobs in Germany were **formerly** employed in the mining industry in the North-East of England.

Q9   naturalism, realism

Q10   b. 'It's amazing', said the lady, 'to see how quickly my little dog is able to bury its bone in the garden'.

Q11   directive

Q12   gain, impart

Q13   faulty, wanting

Q14   knoll: it is a hill – the rest are valleys

Q15   rescinded: it means cancelled – the rest mean late

Q16   dappled

Q17   palpable, manifest

Q18   tedious, enthralling

Q19   expanse: it means a wide-spread-out area – the rest mean a supply beyond sufficiency

Q20   paper, gold

Performance rating

Score 1 point for each completely correct answer.

Total Score	Rating	Percentage of Population
19 / 20	genius level	top 5%
17 / 18	high expert	top 10%
15 / 16	expert	top 30%
13 / 14	high average	top 40%
11 / 12	middle average	top 60%
9 / 10	low average	bottom 40%
7 / 8	borderline low	bottom 30%
5 / 6	low	bottom 10%
0 / 4	very low	bottom 5%

Lexical ability test *(p 46)*

Answers

Q1	blue	**Q16**	light
Q2	year	**Q17**	purl
Q3	moon	**Q18**	rest
Q4	brand	**Q19**	till
Q5	point	**Q20**	fast
Q6	stone	**Q21**	rigmarole
Q7	leader	**Q22**	elemental
Q8	bank	**Q23**	peninsula
Q9	pen	**Q24**	lithesome
Q10	step	**Q25**	auricular
Q11	lap	**Q26**	porcelain
Q12	pitch	**Q27**	resultant
Q13	snarl	**Q28**	unethical
Q14	flight	**Q29**	coruscate
Q15	stake	**Q30**	altimeter

Performance rating

Score 1 point for each correct answer.

Total Score	Rating	Percentage of Population
28 / 30	genius level	top 5%
25 / 27	high expert	top 10%
22 / 24	expert	top 30%
19 / 21	high average	top 40%
15 / 18	middle average	top 60%
12 / 14	low average	bottom 40%
9 / 11	borderline low	bottom 30%
6 / 8	low	bottom 10%
0 / 5	very low	bottom 5%

Numerical aptitude

Numerical sequence test (p 57)

Answers

Q1   112: add 16 each time

Q2   13.5: add 2.7 each time

Q3   76: add 5, 10, 15, 20, 25

Q4   146.41: add 10% each time

Q5   61: less 9, less 6 alternately

Q6   9½: add 1¾ each time

Q7   49: sequence of square numbers; alternatively add 3, 5, 7, 9, 11, 13, 15

Q8   79: less 1, 2, 3, 4, 5, 6, 7

Q9   360: ×1, ×2, ×3 repeated

Q10   61: less 9¾ each time

Q11   106: +7, +14, +21, +28, +35

Q12   29, 64: there are two alternate sequences: the first, starting at 1, adds 7 each time; the second, starting at 100, deducts 9 each time

Q13   216: ×2, ×3, ×2, ×3

Q14   1792: ×2 each time

Q15   16, 31: there are two alternate sequences: the first, starting at the first 1, progresses +3; the second, starting at the second 1, progresses +6

Q16   66.25: deduct 6.75 each time

Q17   31, 87.5: there are two alternate sequences: the first, starting at 100, progresses −2.5; the second, starting at 1, progresses +7.5

Q18   −14, 13: there are two alternate sequences: the first, starting at the first 1, progresses +2; the second, starting at the second 1, progresses −3

Q19   144: +3, ×3 alternately

Q20   −56: deduct 264 each time

Performance rating

Score 1 point for each correct answer.

Total Score	Rating	Percentage of Population
19 / 20	genius level	top 5%
17 / 18	high expert	top 10%
15 / 16	expert	top 30%
13 / 14	high average	top 40%
11 / 12	middle average	top 60%
9 / 10	low average	bottom 40%
7 / 8	borderline low	bottom 30%
5 / 6	low	bottom 10%
0 / 4	very low	bottom 5%

Mathematical calculation test (p 60)

Answers

Q1 B	**Q2** E	**Q3** A	**Q4** C	**Q5** B	**Q6** D	**Q7** C
Q8 A	**Q9** A	**Q10** B	**Q11** D	**Q12** D	**Q13** C	**Q14** B
Q15 D	**Q16** C	**Q17** A	**Q18** D	**Q19** E	**Q20** B	

Performance rating

Score 1 point for each correct answer.

Total Score	Rating	Percentage of Population
19 / 20	genius level	top 5%
17 / 18	high expert	top 10%
15 / 16	expert	top 30%
13 / 14	high average	top 40%
11 / 12	middle average	top 60%
9 / 10	low average	bottom 40%
7 / 8	borderline low	bottom 30%
5 / 6	low	bottom 10%
0 / 4	very low	bottom 5%

Mental arithmetic test (p 66)

Answers

Q1 72	**Q2** 73	**Q3** 67	**Q4** 98	**Q5** 34	**Q6** 72
Q7 24	**Q8** 16	**Q9** 47	**Q10** 675	**Q11** 191	**Q12** 67.5
Q13 2	**Q14** 280	**Q15** 132	**Q16** 69	**Q17** 611	**Q18** 474
Q19 336	**Q20** 203	**Q21** 321	**Q22** 169	**Q23** 676	**Q24** 869
Q25 9929	**Q26** 52	**Q27** 265	**Q28** 234	**Q29** 275	**Q30** 994

Performance rating

Score 1 point for each correct answer.

Total Score	Rating	Percentage of Population
28 / 30	genius level	top 5%
25 / 27	high expert	top 10%
22 / 24	expert	top 30%
19 / 21	high average	top 40%
15 / 18	middle average	top 60%
12 / 14	low average	bottom 40%
9 / 11	borderline low	bottom 30%
6 / 8	low	bottom 10%
0 / 5	very low	bottom 5%

General numerical aptitude test (p 70)

Answers

Q1   3

Q2   5   6   9   1   3

Q3   £130.00:

	originally		now
Stanley	80		
Oliver	50	× 3	150
	130		

Q4   14

Q5 20 minutes:

20 minutes before 12 noon = 11.40

11.40 less 1 hour = 10.40

9 am + (5 × 20) 100 minutes = 10.40

The easiest method of working this out is by logical analysis as follows:

12 noon less 9 am = 180 minutes. 180 minutes less 1 hour = 120 minutes. There is one part before 12 noon and 5 parts after 9 am (6 equal parts in all). 120 ÷ 6 = 20.

Q6 2: average = 5; second-highest odd number = 7

Q7 16: add 0, 1, 2, 3, 4, 5, 6, 7, 8

Q8

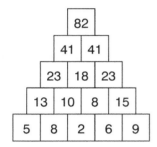

Q9 228: 19 × 12

Q10 21, 67: there are two alternate sequences: the first, starting at the first 5, progresses +2, +4, +8, +16, +32; the second, starting at the second 5, progresses +1, +3, +5, +7

Q11 9 am. If my watch loses 6 minutes per hour, it takes 4 hours to lose 24 minutes, ie when the correct time should be 4 am the watch will show 3.36 (60 − 24 = 36). As this is the time the watch is now showing it must have stopped at 4 am; therefore, the time is now 4 am plus 5 hours = 9 am.

Q12 +: (4 × 8) + 7 = (6 × 3) + (7 × 3)

Q13 22: (13 + 17) − 8 = 22; alternatively (13 + 17) = (22 + 8)

Q14 245: square the numbers in the corner of each triangle and add to obtain the number in the middle: 9^2 (81) + 10^2 (100) + 8^2 (64) = 245

Q15 38: (5 + 14) × 2 = 38

Performance rating

Score 1 point for each correct answer.

Total Score	Rating	Percentage of Population
14 / 15	genius level	top 5%
12 / 13	high expert	top 10%
10 / 11	expert	top 30%
8 / 9	high average	top 40%
6 / 7	middle average	top 60%
4 / 5	low average	bottom 40%
3	borderline low	bottom 30%
2	low	bottom 10%
0 / 1	very low	bottom 5%

Advanced number diagrams test – calculation and logic (p 75)

Answers

Q1   4: 101 (the number formed by the three digits at the top) × 4 = 404 (the number formed by the three digits at the bottom); 152 × 2 = 304; 268 × 3 = 804

Q2   13: 14 + 12 = 26; 26 ÷ 2 = 13

Q3   7: in each circle, the number in the middle is the average of the numbers round the outside

Q4   6: the total of the numbers in each line across and down is 18

Q5   15: in each line divide each of the first two numbers by 4 and then multiply the results to obtain the third number; so 12 ÷ 4 = 3, 20 ÷ 4 = 5, and 3 × 5 = 15

Q6   14: 4 × 7 = 28; 28 ÷ 2 = 14

Q7

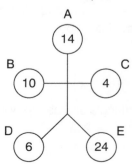

A + B = E; the difference between B and A = C; E ÷ C = D

Q8   46: working clockwise from 1, jump to alternate segments adding 3, 6, 9, 12, 15, 18

Q9

11	23	47

Looking across each line, the numbers progress $\times 2 + 1$, $\times 2 + 1$

Q10   43: numbers in directly opposite circles total 100

Q11   1: numbers in each quadrant plus the connected outer number total 12, for example $4 + 2 + 6$; $5 + 6 + 1$

Q12   360: 45×8

Q13   72, 54: $96 \times 0.75 = 72$; $72 \times 0.75 = 54$

Q14   65: $(6 + 7) \times 5$

Q15   57: looking both across and down, in each line each number is the sum of the previous two

Q16   3: $(2 \times 6) = 12$; $12 \div 4 = 3$

Q17   86: $(6 \times 9) + (8 \times 4)$

Q18   3: the numbers in each of the four hexagons all total 27

Q19   11: in each straight row of four numbers, alternate numbers total the same, for example $(18 + 6) = (10 + 14)$, therefore $(11 + 15) = (4 + 22)$

Q20   39: $(5 \times 7) + 4 = 39$; similarly $(7 \times 4) + 9 = 37$

Performance rating

Score 1 point for each correct answer.

Total Score	Rating	Percentage of Population
19 / 20	genius level	top 5%
17 / 18	high expert	top 10%
15 / 16	expert	top 30%
13 / 14	high average	top 40%
11 / 12	middle average	top 60%
9 / 10	low average	bottom 40%
7 / 8	borderline low	bottom 30%
5 / 6	low	bottom 10%
0 / 4	very low	bottom 5%

Numerical adaptability test (p 84)

Answers

Q1   146: add 5, 10, 15, 20, 25, 30

Q2   720

Q3   37: add 10, 12, 14, 16, 18

Q4   27: the $3 \times 3 \times 3$ cube in the centre

Q5   1: work backwards from 36, that is: 36, 24, 8, 2, 1

Q6   158.5: increase the amount added by 7.5 each time: 7.5, 15, 22.5, 30, 37.5, 45

Q7   15 minutes: 11.45 plus 90 minutes = 1.15

Q8   12: 1 and 5 appear only once; 2 appears four times (the most); $(1 + 5) \times 2 = 12$

Q9   30 miles: 45 mph for 1 hour = 45 miles; for 40 minutes (48 minutes less the 8-minute stop) = $\frac{2}{3}$ of an hour = 30 miles ($\frac{2}{3} \times 45$)

Q10   3½ times: 210 ÷ 60

Performance rating

Score 1 point for each correct answer.

Total Score	Rating	Percentage of Population
9 / 10	genius level	top 5%
8	high expert	top 10%
7	expert	top 30%
6	high average	top 40%
5	middle average	top 60%
4	low average	bottom 40%
3	borderline low	bottom 30%
2	low	bottom 10%
0 / 1	very low	bottom 5%

Geometry test (p 87)

Answers

Q1   B. 4 cm: $4 \times 4 \times 4 = 64$

Q2   C. 40°
The total of the internal angles of a triangle is always 180°, and the total of the two angles on a straight line is always 180°. The value of angle Z (which is a right angle) is 90°. As the value of angle Y must be $180 - 130 = 50°$, the value of angle X must be $180 - (50 + 90) = 40°$.

Q3   B. 108°

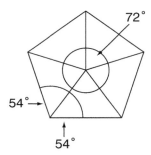

As the total of degrees in a circle is 360, then the value of each of the 5 equal angles in the centre must be $360 \div 5 = 72$. As the internal angles of a triangle always total 180°, the value of the remaining two angles must be $180 - 72 = 108$ (or 54° each). Each internal angle of the pentagon must, therefore, be $54 \times 2 = 108°$.

Q4   D. 720
Each box has a cubic capacity of $1 \times 1 \times 0.5 = 0.5$ cu cm. As the container has a cubic capacity of $10 \times 6 \times 6 = 360$ cu cm, 720 of the smaller boxes $(360 \div 0.5)$ will fit into it.

Q5   A. 125 units: $\frac{150}{12} \times 10$

Q6 D. 22 sq units

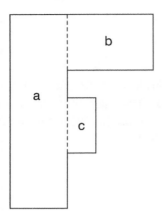

Split the figure into three sections:
Section a = 14 sq units (7 × 2)
Section b = 6 sq units (3 × 2)
Section c = 2 sq unit (1 × 2)
Total: 22 sq units

Q7 C. 9 cm
Each side must be 3 cm (3 × 3 = 9); therefore, three squares placed end to end must form a rectangle with its longest side 3 + 3 + 3 = 9.

Q8 B. 93°

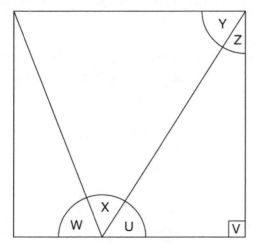

Angle V = 90°, as it is a right angle. Angle Z = 35° (90 – 55), as angle YZ is a right angle. Angle U = 55° (180 – (90 + 35)), as the three angles in a triangle always add up to 180°. Therefore, angle X = 180 – (32 + 55), or 93°, as angle WXU = 180°.

Q9   C. 5 cm

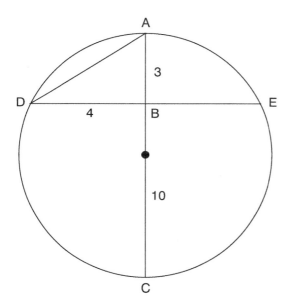

From the information provided, known dimensions can all be determined as above. According to Pythagoras: *The square of the hypotenuse of a right-angled triangle is equal to the sum of the squares of the other two sides.* The length of line AD is, therefore, the square root of $3^2 + 4^2$, or 9 + 16 (25), that is 5.

Q10   E. All of the above can be constructed.

Q11   C. 174 sq cm
The top and bottom would have an area of 3 × 9 = 27 (×2) = 54. The ends would have an area of 3 × 5 = 15 (×2) = 30. The sides would have an area of 5 × 9 = 45 (×2) = 90. Total: 174.

Q12   B. 135 cu cm: 3 × 5 × 9 = 135

Q13   B. 25%: 6 out of the 24 faces are shaded

Q14   C. 254.34: 3.14 × 9^2 or 3.14 × 81 (if the diameter is 18 cm, the radius is 9 cm)

Q15   B. 56.52: 2 × 3.14 × 9

Performance rating

Score 1 point for each correct answer.

Total Score	Rating	Percentage of Population
14 / 15	genius level	top 5%
12 / 13	high expert	top 10%
10 / 11	expert	top 30%
8 / 9	high average	top 40%
6 / 7	middle average	top 60%
4 / 5	low average	bottom 40%
3	borderline low	bottom 30%
2	low	bottom 10%
0 / 1	very low	bottom 5%

Data interpretation test (p 99)

Answers

Questions 1–5

The data may be summarized as follows:

	A	B	C	D	E	F	Total
Year 1	30	15	50	55	20	15	185
Year 2	45	10	70	40	15	20	200

Q1   A: 50%, up from 30 million to 45 million

Q2   E: –25% compared with B –33% and D –28% (approximately)

Q3   F: +33% compared with A +50% and C +40%

Q4   C

Q5   Year 1 +15 million

Questions 6–10

The data may be summarized as follows:

	J	F	M	A	M	J	J	A	S	O	N	D
Town A	110	50	100	150	200	250	100	50	250	300	200	180
Town B	50	80	140	200	50	300	170	190	20	40	100	50
Town C	200	100	150	70	0	250	120	30	0	300	280	100
Town D	250	0	50	300	300	210	0	150	70	200	250	0
Totals	610	230	440	720	550	1010	390	420	340	840	830	330

Q6 B

Q7 February

Q8 Town B: A = 600, B = 710, C = 400, D = 660

Q9 June, October, November

Q10 A

Performance rating

Score 1 point for each completely correct answer.

Total Score	Rating	Percentage of Population
9 / 10	genius level	top 5%
8	high expert	top 10%
7	expert	top 30%
6	high average	top 40%
5	middle average	top 60%
4	low average	bottom 40%
3	borderline low	bottom 30%
2	low	bottom 10%
0 / 1	very low	bottom 5%

Spatial aptitude

Visual odd-one-out test (p 104)

Answers

Q1   D: A is the same as E with black/white dot reversal; similarly B is the same as C.

Q2   F: In all the others the inner arc is a mirror of the larger outer arc, and is directly opposite to it.

Q3   E: It spirals anticlockwise from the middle, whereas all the others spiral clockwise from the middle.

Q4   B: In all the others the circle and triangle are connected.

Q5   B: In all the others all lines start at a corner. In B, one of its lines starts from the middle of one of the sides of the heptagon.

Q6   C: In all the others outer lines are joined to inner broken lines and vice versa.

Q7   F: In all the others the figure in the very centre is repeated on the outside.

Q8   B: All the others have the same string of white/black/white/white/black.

Q9   C: A has the same figures as D, and B has the same figures as E.

Q10   E: The rest are the same figure rotated. E is a mirror image, not a rotation.

Q11   3: The rest have an identical dot arrangement but with black/white reversal: 1 = 8, 2 = 4, 5 = 9 and 6 = 7.

Q12   D: The whirl in the middle is the other way round.

Q13   B: In all the others the arrow is pointing to a black dot.

Q14   A: In all the others the dot is inside the circle.

Q15   D: The rest are all the same figure rotated.

Performance rating

Score 1 point for each correct answer.

Total Score	Rating	Percentage of Population
14 / 15	genius level	top 5%
12 / 13	high expert	top 10%
10 / 11	expert	top 30%
8 / 9	high average	top 40%
6 / 7	middle average	top 60%
4 / 5	low average	bottom 40%
3	borderline low	bottom 30%
2	low	bottom 10%
0 / 1	very low	bottom 5%

Progressive matrices test (p 115)

Answers

Q1 B: Complete and broken lines are continued horizontally and vertically.

Q2 C: Looking across the smaller circle disappears. Looking down, the dot disappears.

Q3 B: Opposite squares contain the diamond in the same position. The circle appears in each of the four corner positions.

Q4 B: Looking across, a larger circle is added. Looking down, the dot disappears.

Q5 B: Looking across, the line moves 45° clockwise. Looking down, it moves 90° clockwise.

Q6 D: Looking across, only the centre dot and circles are carried forward to the third square. Looking down, only the centre dot and lines are carried forward to the third square.

Q7 E: Looking across and down, lines are carried forward to the final square from the first two squares, except when the same lines appear in both of the first two squares, in which case they are cancelled out.

Q8 F: Looking across and down, only the same colour dots that appear in the same position in the first two squares are carried forward to the third square. However, they then change from black to white and vice versa.

Q9 B: Each line across and down contains the letters N, E, W, and in the grid each letter appears the correct way up, on its side and upside down.

Q10 A: Looking across and down, only the same colour figures that appear in the same position in the first two squares are carried forward to the third square. However, they then change from black to white and vice versa.

Q11 C: Looking across, the diamond shape is increasing in size and the dots are in the sequence 3, 2, 1. Looking down, the diamond shape appears at the bottom, on the left side and at the top.

Q12 E: Looking across, a horizontal line is added to the second square and lines appear complete, broken and with a middle gap. Looking down, vertical lines appear in the sequence 1, 2, 3.

Q13 B: The bottom two rows repeat the top two rows, but with the diagonal line between the opposite two corners.

Q14 B: In each line across and down, the dot is in each of the four corners in turn.

Q15 D: Each line across and down contains one each of the four different line/circle arrangements.

Performance rating

Score 1 point for each correct answer.

Total Score	Rating	Percentage of Population
14 / 15	genius level	top 5%
12 / 13	high expert	top 10%
10 / 11	expert	top 30%
8 / 9	high average	top 40%
6 / 7	middle average	top 60%
4 / 5	low average	bottom 40%
3	borderline low	bottom 30%
2	low	bottom 10%
0 / 1	very low	bottom 5%

Visual analogy test (p 128)

Answers

Q1   B: The figures change places, and also change from black to white and vice versa.

Q2   E: The square on the left goes to the bottom of the new arrangement, the square middle left goes to the top of the new arrangement, the figure on the right goes to middle left, and the figure middle right goes to middle right.

Q3   D: The symbol top left goes to bottom left, the symbol top right goes to bottom right, the symbol bottom left goes to top right and the symbol bottom right goes to top left.

Q4   D: All dots on the inside transfer to the outside and vice versa. All black dots become white and vice versa.

Q5   D: The line rotates 90° anticlockwise. The larger internal circle moves to the centre and the smaller black circle goes inside it.

Q6   B: Lines are transferred from inside the first two rectangles to the third rectangle, except where two lines appear in the same position, in which case they are cancelled out.

Q7   C: Black triangles change to white circles and vice versa. White triangles change to black circles and vice versa.

Q8   E: There are three styles of arrow. The arrow at the end transfers to the beginning, but points in the same direction as the style of arrow originally in that position. Similarly the arrow at the beginning transfers to the centre, and the arrow in the centre transfers to the end.

Q9 E: All three components flip over and change black to white and vice versa.

Q10 C: The top horizontal line of the first figure is removed and the bottom horizontal line of the second figure is removed.

Q11 D: The top right corner is folded inwards.

Q12 C: The figure at the bottom (the parallelogram) rotates 90°. The figure at the top (the square) increases in size and goes inside the parallelogram. The figure in the middle (the rectangle) rotates 90°, reduces in size and goes inside the square.

Q13 B: The figure in the middle moves over the figure on the right. The figure on the extreme left moves to the extreme right.

Q14 E: Only the line that appears in the same position inside the first three squares just once is carried forward to the final square.

Q15 C: The dot in the middle transfers to outside the ellipse on the right. The lines inside the ellipse all rotate 180°.

Performance rating

Score 1 point for each correct answer.

Total Score	Rating	Percentage of Population
14 / 15	genius level	top 5%
12 / 13	high expert	top 10%
10 / 11	expert	top 30%
8 / 9	high average	top 40%
6 / 7	middle average	top 60%
4 / 5	low average	bottom 40%
3	borderline low	bottom 30%
2	low	bottom 10%
0 / 1	very low	bottom 5%

Visual sequence test (p 139)

Answers

Q1   D: The base of the triangle moves clockwise round the pentagon at each stage, first by one side, then two sides, then three and finally four.

Q2   E: At each stage the white circle moves two corners clockwise and the black dot moves one corner anticlockwise.

Q3   A: The line moves 45° clockwise at each stage and alternates straight/curved.

Q4   C: The corner line moves round one corner clockwise at each stage, and the corner section formed alternates white/black. The line arrangements appear in pairs, first one line vertical/horizontal, then two lines vertical/horizontal and then three lines.

Q5   B: The first three figures are being repeated, but only the left half.

Q6   F: The largest arc moves 90° clockwise at each stage, the middle arc moves 180° and the inner arc moves 90° clockwise.

Q7   D: The dot moves down a space/figure. When the dot appears in a figure, that figure turns upside down.

Q8   F: The top and bottom arms both rotate 45° at each stage.

Q9   F: The first three figures are being repeated but rotated 180° clockwise. The dot alternates black/white.

Q10   D: The black square and line originally at the top are moving down one row at a time. The line and black square originally at the right and left of the middle row are moving from right to left and left to right respectively one column at each stage. In D the lines and black squares occupy the same positions, and therefore the lines are obscured by the black squares.

Q11   D: At each stage the dot moves one corner clockwise and the curved line moves from corner to opposite corner at each stage.

Q12   D: The dot moves from corner to corner clockwise and alternates white/black.

Q13   A: There are two alternate sequences. In the first, a larger circle is added at each stage. In the second, the largest circle is removed at each stage.

Q14   C: At each stage another figure is added to the next corner, working clockwise. The figure added alternates white/black.

Q15   E: The dot moves one corner/two corners clockwise and appears white/black in turn.

Performance rating

Score 1 point for each correct answer.

Total Score	Rating	Percentage of Population
14 / 15	genius level	top 5%
12 / 13	high expert	top 10%
10 / 11	expert	top 30%
8 / 9	high average	top 40%
6 / 7	middle average	top 60%
4 / 5	low average	bottom 40%
3	borderline low	bottom 30%
2	low	bottom 10%
0 / 1	very low	bottom 5%

Shapes test (p 148)

Answers

Q1   C

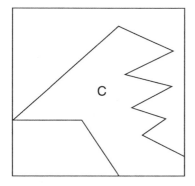

Q2   A and E
Q3   E
Q4   C

Q5   D

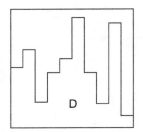

Q6   D
Q7   D

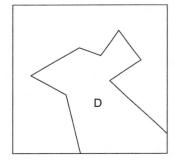

Q8   B and C
Q9   C
Q10 A

Performance rating

Score 1 point for each completely correct answer.

Total Score	Rating	Percentage of Population
9 / 10	genius level	top 5%
8	high expert	top 10%
7	expert	top 30%
6	high average	top 40%
5	middle average	top 60%
4	low average	bottom 40%
3	borderline low	bottom 30%
2	low	bottom 10%
0 / 1	very low	bottom 5%

General IQ tests

Test one (p 161)

Answers

Q1 dialogue

Q2 sumptuous

Q3 deference, respect

Q4 animal, verse

Q5 potent, weak

Q6 critical, appreciative

Q7 preacher

Q8 culminate: it means end – the rest mean begin

Q9 The personnel were all presented with their personal stationery.

Q10 As she became older and wiser she was able to teach many of her high moral principles to her pupils, who were quite grateful to her for the rest of their lives.

Q11 B

Q12 123

Q13 1.4

Q14 E

Q15 Jack 68, Jill 51
Jack = 4/3, Jill = 3/3; total = 7/3; 119/7 = 17; Jack = 4 × 17 = 68, and Jill = 3 × 17 = 51

Q16 27: 3 numbers = 19 × 3 = 57; 2 numbers = 15 × 2 = 30; the third number is, therefore, 57 – 30 = 27

Q17 1, –14: deduct 1, 3, 5, 7, 9, 11, 13, 15

Q18 210

Q19 Sid £270.00, Mary £180.00
Divide 450 into 5 parts = 90. Sid has 3 parts (3 × 90) and Mary has 2 parts (2 × 90).

Q20 6

Q21 B: Looking down, a triangle is added on the right side of each box. Looking across, the triangle on the left side increases in size.

Q22 A: The line moves one corner clockwise. The white dot moves two corners clockwise.

Q23 E: At each stage, a dot is added, working clockwise. Dots added alternate white/black.

Q24   D: Looking across, the lines rotate 45° anticlockwise in each line. Looking down, they rotate 45° clockwise in each column.

Q25   E: The rest are all the same figure rotated.

Q26   B: At each stage, a new line is added, working round the sides clockwise. At the stage after being added, all lines become broken.

Q27   A: In each row and column there are a white dot, a black dot, a bottom horizontal line and one triangle inverted.

Q28   C

Q29   C: At each stage the pairs of arrows are rotating 45°, the first clockwise and the second anticlockwise.

Q30   C: So that it appears in the largest circle and the isosceles triangle.

Performance rating

Score 1 point for each correct answer.

Total Score	Rating	Percentage of Population
28 / 30	genius level	top 5%
25 / 27	high expert	top 10%
22 / 24	expert	top 30%
19 / 21	high average	top 40%
15 / 18	middle average	top 60%
12 / 14	low average	bottom 40%
9 / 11	borderline low	bottom 30%
6 / 8	low	bottom 10%
0 / 5	very low	bottom 5%

Test two (p 170)

Answers

Q1   salutary, beneficial

Q2   verdant

Q3   inept

Q4   lethal, innocuous

Q5   quorum: quorum is the minimum number of people necessary in order for a meeting to take place – the rest are all types of meeting

Q6   spiral

Q7   legalistic, strict

Q8   dispute

Q9   thermostat: it is an instrument for maintaining a constant temperature – the rest are specifically measuring instruments

Q10 C

'Who's left this on my desk?' exclaimed the headmaster. 'Whose chewing gum is it? Come on now, answer me at once, to whom does it belong?'

Q11 76, 114: the numbers are increasing by 19

Q12 17.5 days: The time for five men is 140 (5 × 28) man days. Eight men, therefore, take 140 ÷ 8 = 17.5 days.

Q13 2160, 6480: ×2, ×3, ×2, ×3 etc

Q14 21 cm: (26.5 ÷ 10.6) × 8.4

Q15 35%

12 out of 48 = 12/48 = 25%

18 out of 30 = 18/30 = 60%

Q16 36: add 0, 1, 2, 3, 4, 5, 6, 7

Q17 86: subtract 0.5, 1, 1.5, 2, 2.5, 3, 3.5

Q18 A

Q19 108: add 36 each time

Q20

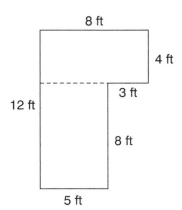

8 × 4 = 32 sq feet; 8 × 5 = 40 sq feet; total: 72 sq feet × £10.65 = £766.80

Q21 D: Looking across, the dot changes from white to black. Looking down, a vertical line is added.

Q22 B: To complete the four shields.

Q23 C: At each stage, the small hand moves 135° clockwise, and the long hand moves 45° anticlockwise.

Q24 B: In all the others, the triangle and square overlap.

Q25 D: The first analogy is reversed. The circle reduces in size and goes to the top, the square increases in size and goes in the middle and the diamond rotates 90° and goes at the bottom.

Q26 D: Looking across, all lines go inside the figure. Looking down, the figures are circle, triangle, square, and the lines increase 1, 2, 3.

Q27 A

Q28 A: The bottom line repeats the top line in reverse, except complete lines become broken, and vice versa.

Q29 E: There are two separate white dots and two chains: black/white/black and white/black/white.

Q30 A: Reversing the first analogy, the four small squares become one large square, and the cross goes inside it.

Performance rating

Score 1 point for each correct answer.

Total Score	Rating	Percentage of Population
28 / 30	genius level	top 5%
25 / 27	high expert	top 10%
22 / 24	expert	top 30%
19 / 21	high average	top 40%
15 / 18	middle average	top 60%
12 / 14	low average	bottom 40%
9 / 11	borderline low	bottom 30%
6 / 8	low	bottom 10%
0 / 5	very low	bottom 5%

In addition to the above general performance rating, scores should be analysed for each of the three separate subsections in each test – verbal aptitude, numerical aptitude and spatial aptitude. This will give a clear indication of current strengths and weaknesses. These can then be worked on and improved according to the general analysis sections for verbal aptitude, numerical aptitude and spatial aptitude (see 'Interpretations of your test scores').

The performance rating in respect of each 10-question subsection is as follows. Score 1 point for each correct answer.

Total Score	Rating	Percentage of Population
9 / 10	genius level	top 5%
8	high expert	top 10%
7	expert	top 30%
6	high average	top 40%
5	middle average	top 60%
4	low average	bottom 40%
3	borderline low	bottom 30%
2	low	bottom 10%
0 / 1	very low	bottom 5%

CHAPTER 7

Interpretations of your test scores

Verbal aptitude – general analysis

The performance ratings in each of the tests of verbal aptitude will provide a clear indication of strengths and weaknesses in the different disciplines being tested. This is important, as it is likely that, even though you may have a high overall verbal aptitude, there will be some tests on which you have scored more highly than on other tests. It is, therefore, important to analyse individual scores, which will enable you to build and capitalize on your strengths and work on improving performance in areas of weakness.

An analysis of the scores obtained in each of the tests will also provide you with an indication of your overall verbal ability:

- *Majority of scores in the high average range or above.* Possessing a good vocabulary, if put to good use, will determine the quality of your ability to communicate both orally and in writing. You have good to excellent verbal skills and understanding, and should consider capitalizing on these skills career-wise.

People who possess a level of verbal skills often excel in fields such as writing (author, journalist, editing, critic), teaching (language, drama), legal profession (judge, barrister, lawyer) and personnel work (advocate, human resources, counsellor) and as actors, psychologists, interpreters and interviewers.

- *Majority of scores in the middle average range.* Whilst you have generally good verbal skills and are likely to have a way with words there are obviously areas in which there is some room for improvement. It is worth bearing in mind that as there is no ceiling to knowledge it is possible with practice and commitment to increase verbal skills considerably.

  An analysis of scores obtained on the various tests in this section will identify which areas of verbal aptitude are most in need of further practice and improvement.

- *Majority of scores in the low average to below range.* Whilst you may have a general ability to communicate effectively your score indicates that verbal aptitude is not currently one of your strengths and to a great extent you do not have sufficient command of many of the subtle differences between words.

  It is recommended that you analyse carefully the results obtained from each of the above tests in order to identify areas of specific weakness.

There are several ways in which you are able to improve your verbal skills:

- Find the time to practise and practise again on tests similar to the ones contained in the section on verbal aptitude.

- Analyse carefully the questions you answered incorrectly in the tests. If you are in doubt as to the meaning of any word, look it up in a dictionary or thesaurus.

- Read as much as you possibly can. If you have neither the time nor inclination to read a book from cover to cover, read extracts. Try to read a magazine or newspaper at least once every day.

- Join a public library, browse the shelves and borrow some books. Reading is learning!

- Select a word at random from a passage in a book or magazine. Try to think of other words similar in meaning. Then try to think of words that have the opposite meaning.

- Think about the context in which words are used. By far the majority of word meanings are learnt from hearing them or reading them in a certain context.

- Be curious! Be enquiring! If you are unsure about the meaning of a word you have heard or read, then ask, or look up its meaning as soon as you get the opportunity.

- Try word games such as crossword puzzles, Scrabble or word associations. Start with easier crossword puzzles and gradually build up to harder ones. For any clues that you cannot solve, check the answers first before discarding the puzzle completely.

Numerical aptitude – general analysis

The performance ratings in each of the above tests will provide a clear indication of strengths and weaknesses in the different disciplines being tested. This is important, as it is likely that, even though you may have a high overall numerical aptitude, there will be some tests on which you have scored more highly than on other tests. It is, therefore, important to analyse individual scores, which will enable you to build and capitalize on your strengths and work on improving performance in areas of weakness.

An analysis of the scores obtained in each of the tests will also provide you with an indication of your overall numerical ability:

- *Majority of scores in the high average range or above.* You have a good to excellent firm knowledge of basic arithmetic and are able to apply this knowledge analytically and effectively with the result that you come up with a high percentage of correct solutions. Because good numerical aptitude is one of your strengths you should consider capitalizing on these skills career-wise.

  Good mathematical ability is an excellent stepping stone to career success in jobs such as accounting or banking. If you have a high degree of aptitude for geometry then success could follow in careers such as graphic designing or architecture. People who possess a high level of numerical skills also often excel in jobs such as auditor, business consultant, financial analyst, mathematics or science teacher, quantity surveyor, tax adviser, company secretary, computer programmer or stockbroker.

- *Majority of scores in the middle average range.* Whilst you generally have good mathematical skills and the ability (which is not necessarily the same as resolve) to manage your own financial affairs satisfactorily, there are obviously areas in which there is some room for improvement.

  An analysis of scores obtained on the various tests in this section will identify which areas of numerical aptitude are most in need of further practice and improvement.

- *Majority of scores in the low average to below range.* Whilst you may have a rudimentary grasp of arithmetic your score indicates that numerical aptitude is not currently one of your strengths.

  It is recommended that you analyse carefully the results obtained from each of the above tests in order to identify areas of specific weakness.

There are several ways in which you are able to improve your numerical skills, including some exercises you can perform every day:

- Practise as much as you can on the tests in this book and on any similar tests you can find either on the internet or in a public library.

- Next time you need to do a calculation, try working it out in your head first. Then use your calculator to see whether or not you were correct.

- Next time you visit the supermarket try to estimate the cost of the items in your shopping trolley.

- Learn to think numerically. Next time you pay for some goods, calculate the amount of change in your head. For example, if the cost of goods is £36.73 and you give the sales assistant four £10 notes, calculate quickly in your head the amount of change you should receive from the cashier.

- Do not be afraid of numbers. The more you practise, the more proficient you will become.

- If you are quoted a price less value added tax (VAT), learn to calculate the VAT in your head.

Spatial aptitude – general analysis

As spatial aptitude involves quite different thought processes to those that determine verbal or numerical aptitude it is quite common for people who score very highly on numerical and verbal aptitude tests to score equally badly on spatial aptitude tests and vice versa.

This is because the left side of the human brain is analytical and functions in a sequential and logical fashion and is the side that controls language, academic studies and rationality. The right side of the brain is creative and intuitive and leads, for example, to the birth of ideas for works of art and music and is the side of the brain that determines how well we are able to adapt to tests of spatial aptitude. As many people have some degree of brain bias, they thus perform better on tests that involve thought processes controlled by the stronger side of their brain.

People who scored badly on the tests in this section, after performing well on the verbal and numerical aptitude tests, should, therefore, have no great cause for concern. They have, however, the opportunity to practise and increase their performance on this type of spatial aptitude testing and to develop their right-brain thinking.

The performance ratings in each of the above tests will provide a clear indication of strengths and weaknesses in the different disciplines being tested. This is important, as it is likely that, even though you may have a high or low overall spatial aptitude, there will be some tests on which you have scored more highly than on other tests. It is, therefore, important to analyse individual scores, which will enable you to build and capitalize on your strengths and work on improving performance in areas of weakness.

An analysis of the scores obtained in each of the tests will also provide you with an indication of your overall spatial ability:

- *Majority of scores in the high average range or above*. You have a good to excellent spatial and abstract reasoning ability. This indicates that you are likely to have a strongly intuitive, inventive, enquiring and creative nature and an appreciation of the arts. Spatial aptitude is also useful when it comes to everyday activities such as reading a map or fitting things into suitcases. Because good spatial aptitude is one of your strengths you should consider capitalizing on these skills career-wise.

  People with a high degree of spatial intelligence like to think in images and tend to see the big picture rather than the component parts. Also, once an image has been formed in the mind they are then able to manipulate this image in their mind and imagine many different results. This is particularly valuable to professionals such as architects, sculptors, engineers and designers.

People who possess a high level of spatial aptitude often excel in fields such as architecture, photography, engineering, design and decorating, and as artists, carpenters, landscape designers, cartoon animators, guides, fashion designers, shop fitters and civil engineers.

- *Majority of scores in the middle average range.* Whilst you generally have a reasonably good level of spatial aptitude there are obviously areas in which there is some room for improvement.

An analysis of scores obtained on the various tests in this section will identify which areas of spatial aptitude are most in need of further practice and improvement. Spatial aptitude is something that can, fortunately, be improved with practice. We all have the ability to be imaginative and creative. Often, though, the creative side to our brain can be neglected at the expense of the more analytical left-hand side. It is, however, of enormous advantage to use both sides of the brain in equal measure. For example, when you are able to perceive the big picture and the essential details simultaneously you are likely to possess the verbal and numerical skills to translate your intuition into an understandable, realistic and workable reality.

- *Majority of scores in the low average to below range.* As the majority of your scores in the tests in this section indicate that spatial aptitude is not currently one of your strengths, it is recommended that in the first instance you analyse carefully the results obtained from each of the tests in order to identify areas of specific weakness.

It may be you have low pattern recognition skills, which means that you find difficulty in recognizing underlying mechanisms of various contraptions, or fail to appreciate connections between implements or events or make sense of scrambled data.

It is, however, possible to increase your spatial ability and skills considerably. There are several ways in which you are able to do this, including some exercises you can perform every day:

- Keep practising on the tests in this book and on any similar tests you can find in the library or on the internet. The more you practise the better you become. Constant practice can bring about considerable improvement as well as increasing your general spatial awareness.

- The next time you take a long journey take on the responsibility for reading and providing directions.

- When packing things into a box or suitcase, don't just throw things in haphazardly. Think of the most efficient way they will fit, thus using the space available most effectively.

- Don't be overawed! At first glance questions such as the ones in this section may appear daunting but the secret is not to give up too quickly. Try again to solve some of the questions in this section. If you cannot solve them, have a second look some time later. Often the solution will come to you seemingly out of the blue but in reality it is because the brain has been given the opportunity to process the information further. So, already, you are putting your brain to work in a different way, and developing right-brain thinking.

Personality testing

Test 1 – structured or flexible

This test is designed to measure whether you prefer to organize your life in a structured way by making decisions or in a flexible way by discovering life as you go along.

The organizing of your life in a structured way, in which you prefer to know exactly where you stand, is referred to as *judgement*. If the flexible approach is preferred then this is referred to as *perception*.

People who prefer the structured approach prefer their life to be well organized and continually to make carefully considered decisions about, for example, who they meet, what they say and what they do, and not to rush into things haphazardly.

Keywords: structured, firm, controlled, decisive

On the other hand people who prefer the flexible approach are more comfortable when keeping their options open at all times and not being bound or restricted by an organized or fixed routine. Such people tend in their lifestyle to be continually finding out more and experiencing new things, and are not afraid of changes of direction in their lifestyle.

Keywords: flexible, inquisitive, spontaneous, open, meandering

Total score 55–75: markedly flexible
Total score 40–54: no marked preponderance demonstrated either way
Total score less than 40: markedly structured

Test 2 – social intelligence

Social intelligence, also commonly referred to as 'people skills', is the ability to relate to, understand and interact effectively with others on a daily basis.

People with a high level of social intelligence, therefore, have the ability to get along with other people and are very much at ease in society in general. They are also able to react well to stimuli from other members of a group, as well as having the ability to recognize or identify temporary moods or underlying personality traits of strangers.

It is becoming increasingly accepted that social intelligence is as important as, or even more important than, a high-measured IQ.

Award yourself 2 points for every 'c' answer, 1 point for every 'a' and 0 points for every 'b'.

Total score 45–50: exceptionally high social intelligence factor
Total score 40–44: very high social intelligence factor
Total score 36–39: high social intelligence factor
Total score 32–35: well above average social intelligence factor
Total score 26–31: above average social intelligence factor
Total score 22–25: average social intelligence factor
Total score 19–21: below average social intelligence factor
Total score below 19: low social intelligence factor

Test 3 – team effectiveness and leadership

There are many factors to take into account when considering what will make a good team and what will make a good team member. These may be summarized as follows:

- *Motivation.* What makes us do anything? Motivation may be lacking if the purpose of the team is not clearly defined and is not in line with all team members' aspirations.

- *Camaraderie.* Camaraderie encourages openness, fellowship and loyalty. A team is at its most effective when all its members are supportive of each other and pulling together in the same direction.

- *Interest.* Interest and motivation will diminish unless the team think the work is important and that the mission is clear.

- *Challenge.* People usually respond to challenge in a positive way. Challenge is in itself a motivator. The greater the challenge, the greater the effort.

The best team leaders are able to create the right conditions in which the team is able to motivate itself, as well as having a clear understanding of what makes a good team player.

A good team leader must also understand the importance of the team's purpose and challenges, at the same time focusing on maintaining camaraderie, responsibility and growth.

Award yourself 2 points for every 'b' answer, 1 point for every 'c' and 0 points for every 'a'.

32–40 points: good leadership qualities
20–31 points: possible leadership qualities
Less than 20: low leadership qualities

With over 1,000 titles in printed and digital format, **Kogan Page** offers affordable, sound business advice

www.koganpage.com